D0725844

To Love and Be Loved by Jesus

Meditation and Commentary on the Gospel of Mark

Alfred McBride, O. Praem.

Our Sunday Visitor Publishing Division
Our Sunday Visitor, Inc.
Huntington, Indiana 46750

Nihil Obstat: Reverend Richard J. Murphy, O.M.I.
               Censor Deputatus

Imprimatur: Reverend Msgr. William J. Kane, V.G.
               Vicar General for the Archdiocese of Washington
               July 16, 1991

The nihil obstat and imprimatur are official declarations that a book or pamphlet is free of doctrinal or moral error. No implication is contained therein that those who have granted the nihil obstat and the imprimatur agree with the content, opinions or statements expressed.

ISBN: 0-87973-356-X
LCCCN: 91-62162

PRINTED IN THE UNITED STATES OF AMERICA

Cover design by Rebecca J. Heaston
Editorial production by Kelley L. Renz
356

To Love and Be Loved by Jesus

Meditation and Commentary on the Gospel of Mark

Dedicated to Catherine Corcoran Dougherty,
May God bless her.

About the cover:

As I looked, a stormwind came from the North, a huge cloud with flashing fire [enveloped in brightness], from the midst of which [the midst of the fire] something gleamed like electrum. Within it were figures resembling four living creatures that looked like this: their form was human, but each had four faces and four wings, and their legs went straight down; the soles of their feet were round. They sparkled with a gleam like burnished bronze.
Their faces were like this: each of the four had the face of a man, but on the right side was the face of a lion, and on the left side the face of an ox, and finally each had the face of an eagle....

—Ezekiel 1:4-8

The four living creatures seen by Ezekiel in the vision described above are believed to symbolize the four authors of the gospels. St. Mark is symbolized by the lion because he begins his gospel with an account of John the Baptist, roaring in the wilderness, announcing the coming of the Messiah.

Contents

tion to eliminate this inner tension by renouncing one or another of these two orientations ... to be content with a subjective interpretation which is wrongly called "spiritual," or a scientific interpretation which makes the texts "sterile."

—English Edition of *L'Osservatore Romano*, April 22, 1991

This commentary/meditation which you are about to read was written with this total vision in mind. You will not find it heavily scientific because it was not meant to be a popularization of the scientific methods of interpretation. At the same time, it is meant to reflect the beneficial results of scientific studies. You will discover it is aimed at opening up the person, message, and work of Jesus Christ whose work of salvation in union with the Father and the Holy Spirit is presented. Therefore, Jesus centered and faith growth envisioned.

It is my hope that these reflections will draw you to love the Bible, and in so doing, love Christ, yourself, and others. We are thus loving more than a book or sacred texts, we are in a total love affair. Perhaps Chaim Potok's description of the "Dance of the Torah" has something to say to us here. The scene is a Hasidic Synagogue in the Williamsburg section of Brooklyn. A religious festival is in progress and the participants have reached a part of the ceremony where scrolls of the Torah are passed around and certain privileged members are allowed to dance with it. We pick up the scene as the principal character, who has been agonizing about his faith and its relation to life, is handed the scroll.

"I held the scroll as something precious to me, a living being with whose soul I was forever bound, this Sacred Scroll, this Word, this Fire of God, this Source for my own creation, this velvet encased Fountain of All Life which I now clasped in a passionate embrace. I danced with the Torah for a long time, following the line of dancers through the steamy air of the synagogue and out into the chill tumultuous street and back into the synagogue and then reluctantly yielding the scroll to a huge dark-bearded man who hungrily scooped it up and swept away with it in his arms."

—*The Gift of Asher Lev*, paperback, p. 351

Should not our encounter with Scripture be a dance with the Holy Word?

There was an old folk custom, now lost in the mists of history, in which a child was formally introduced to the sweetness of the Word of God. A page of the Bible was given to the child. Upon the page was spread some honey and the child was asked to taste it. Hence from earliest youth, the child would be introduced to a positive experience of Scripture, the sweetness of the Word of God.

What else need be said?

"How sweet are thy words to my taste,
sweeter than honey to my mouth" (Ps. 119:103, RSV).

Introduction: Mark the Storyteller

Shakespearean actor Alec McCowen has been performing a one-man show, featuring St. Mark's gospel for over ten years. When he first conceived the idea of doing a one-man show, he thought of duplicating efforts like those done about Mark Twain, Emily Dickinson, and Harry Truman. Then it struck him that he could do a gospel. He tried St. John, but found the material too symbolic and theological. Matthew had a good story, but was too long. Luke possessed great beauty but the aesthetics slowed down the pace of the story. Only Mark was short enough, straightforward, and blessed with a quick-paced story line.

McCowen said that when he set about memorizing the text of St. Mark's gospel, he took over two hours to master the first verse. He did not need that much time to remember the words, but rather the feeling, the tone, the right note that would release the music of the remaining verses.

He chose the noble prose of the King James version of the Bible. That was a text translated for public reading, a text born in the golden age of Elizabethan prose, a rendering of the story that sings with the rhythm of the English language. On the lips of a superb actor like McCowen, the rolling cadences of Mark's gospel have never sounded so good, except perhaps in the original language. Homilists, preachers and liturgical readers could reap great benefits from attending a McCowen performance of Mark. He is an excellent model for how to proclaim the sacred text with intelligence, feeling, and simplicity.

Amazingly, McCowen is able to deliver the antique words (hath's, wast's, thou's) in such a way that their forbidding (to some modern ears) eccentricity never intrudes on the flow of the meaning. His stage setting echoes the minimalist narrative of Mark. The audience sees a table on which is a book stand, a pitcher of water, and a glass. A chair is set behind the table. The regular stage curtains complete the simple scene. The actor wears an open necked shirt, a floppy pullover sweater, cord pants, and scuffed loafers.

This spartan presentation and setting makes the words of Mark bear the dramatic burden. McCowen avoids histrionics, highs and lows, and dramatic whispers. His delivery is plain and relaxed, becoming animated in the various dialogues that occur in the story. The finished product is affecting, producing zingers, small crescendos, and a cumulative effect that creates a wonderful sense of release at the conclusion of the gospel. A viewer-listener gets the sense that one has been listening to Mark himself. The impact makes one realize why the very proclamation of the Scripture was itself so provocative, persuasive, and liberating.

This meditation and commentary on Mark's gospel attempts to capture that same spirit. The story line receives major attention. Historical, geographical, and cultural comments are added where it seems useful for the understanding of the story. The same is true for meditative reflections. In all cases the reason for re-telling the Marcan gospel is to invite the reader to love and be loved by Jesus Christ. The purpose of this book will be fulfilled if the reader is motivated to a conversion of heart that leads him or her to a life that is less anxious, a mind that is less suspicious, a heart that is less hostile.

Mark wrote the shortest gospel, but one that includes more vivid details than either Matthew or Luke. He writes like an eyewitness, though he was not. Tradition claims that Mark obtained many of these details from Peter. The other gospels say that Jesus took a child and set him in their midst. Mark has Jesus taking the child into his arms. It is Mark who describes the 5,000 to be fed as sitting on green grass — and just at sundown. He notes that during the storm at sea, the sleeping Jesus rested his head on a cushion. A gifted story teller, Mark moves the reader right along, portraying a resolute Jesus determined to let people know the Good News about God's kingdom of love, justice, and mercy breaking into the life of every man and woman.

In our day, we struggle to encounter the human side of Jesus. We can find no better gospel than Mark's for experiencing the human Jesus. Mark is comfortable simply saying Jesus was a carpenter, a village businessman. Matthew draws back from that and pictures Jesus as the son of a carpenter, as if to avoid identifying Jesus as a worker. Forcefully, Mark describes the Spirit as "driving" Jesus into the desert for the temptation. Matthew and Luke take a less blunt approach and report that the Spirit "led" Jesus there.

If ever we wanted to know about the emotions of Jesus, Mark offers us a satisfying profile of a Jesus who was as emotional as any of us. In his gospel, Jesus sighs, groans, feels compassion, marvels, gets mad, and openly shows affection for people. Mark gives us a Jesus who could be worn out, hungry, and yearning for a nap. The human face of Jesus glows in the Marcan narrative.

At the same time, Mark never ignores the mystery of Christ's divinity. In the very first verse, Mark speaks of Jesus as the Son of God. He matches this declaration of faith with the testimony of the Centurion near the end of his gospel, when that Roman soldier says that Jesus was truly the Son of God. Repeatedly, Mark uses the terms amazement, wonder, awe, and astonishment to characterize people's reactions after Jesus performs miracles and delivers teachings that reflect his divine origin and identity. It will be clear from this commentary that these reactions to Jesus were "pre-faith" events. Jesus will not be satisfied to astound others. Jesus will want faith in himself, the total Christ, both God and man. He is not a mere wonder-worker astonishing the crowds; he is a Savior come to redeem and love and forgive all who come to him in faith.

In a variety of ways Mark pictures Jesus as forming disciples and calling people to discipleship. Central to this is Christ's challenge to deny the self, take the Cross, and follow him (cf. Mark 8:34-38). While his whole gospel describes the various beliefs, attitudes, and practices required of a disciple, no passage is more forthright and no other so unambiguous.

Mark places this discipleship text at dead center of his gospel, stripping away any illusions that otherwise might be indulged. Our relationship to Christ will not be that of a student with a teacher, but one of a disciple and a master. A student need not have any personal commitment to a teacher. A disciple is meant not only to believe what the master says, but must enter into a bond as profound as love and a behavior as challenging as the master's.

Disciples will not have the luxury of a self preservation attitude toward their lives and powers. They will not be allowed the caution that protects the self from giving one's life to the last drop. Jesus will demonstrate the grand passion with which he marches the royal road of the cross. He expects no less of his disciples. Only when the disciple "loses" his or her life by pouring it out with enthusiasm and love, is life really "gained."

In Mark's gospel, passions flare up, emotions stir, and convictions are shown unblushingly. His narrative starts and bursts like a rushing stream. Note how often he uses the term "immediately." Mark is not a timid writer, faintly outlining a relatively interesting story. Mark wants to push and shove his way into the attention of the reader. That does not mean he wants to force belief, love, and commitment, no more than the Jesus he characterizes. It does mean that he is a determined attention getter.

Mark is by no means the contemplative John the evangelist, nor the stately institutional Matthew, nor yet the lovely artist Luke. He is more like an earthy peasant who is impatient with theological niceties, organizational preoccupations, or aesthetic attractiveness. He rallies the instincts of common sense to convert the reader to Jesus. He gets to the point right away and discards the ceremonies of approach that others may use — and need.

Mark appeals to the straightforward in all of us, weary of the obliqueness of everyday life, frustrated with the mirrors so many use to distract us from getting at truth. At first sight he may not seem very loveable, but after a time he grows on us. More accurately, his Jesus grows on us. After all, that is the point of any gospel.

1   The Dove and the Leper

A Master of Ceremonies and a Guest of Honor (Mk. 1:1-13)

The human spirit hungers for a person who can witness God's presence. Traditionally, biblical prophets answered that need. Four centuries had passed since God's people heard a prophet. Then came the voice at the Jordan, awakening vivid memories of Elijah and assuring people that God had not forgotten them.

The Jordan flows from the lake of Galilee in the north to the Dead Sea in the south. Ancients called it the "liquid backbone of Palestine." In summer the heat rises to 118 degrees, but in winter, a gentler climate favors the growth of grass and wild flowers on Jordan's banks. Several fords exist — shallow spots where people can wade across the river. Joshua crossed this historic river leading the Israelites forward to conquer this Promised Land.

Now comes John the Baptist to a ford in the Jordan to ask people to conquer their sinfulness and enter the Promised Land of salvation. While the exact spot the Baptist chose is not known, tradition has selected one not far from Jericho. Caravans favored this ford for their crossings.

Where did John receive his calling? What training did he have? Born of a priest and a saintly mother, John experienced the presence of God even in his mother's womb. Elizabeth tells Mary, "For at the moment the sound of your greeting reached my ears, the infant in my womb leaped for joy" (Lk. 1:44). God marked the boy from the beginning to be his prophet.

No gospel record says anything about his training years. Since the Qumran monastery is only about ten miles from the place John began his Jordan ministry, some have wondered if he may have spent time with that community. Though nothing can be proved, the comparisons are striking. The priestly community of Qumran would have been partial to admitting the son of a priest, as John was.

The Dead Sea Scrolls tell us much about this holy community, housed in a desert monastery by the Dead Sea. They saw themselves as Isaiah's voice of God crying out for spiritual renewal from their desert pulpit (Is. 40:3). John claimed the same calling and identified himself as exactly that voice asking people to prepare for the imminent arrival of the Lord.

At Qumran, they prized prayer and fasting. John also pursued the ascetical life. At Qumran, the members took frequent ritual baths — or baptisms — to symbolize their quest for moral purity. John called for only one water cleansing, one baptism from him, to get ready for the messianic baptism in the Holy Spirit.

John differed from the monks in one major aspect. They had become a monastic elite. They huddled together far from the world and took a superior attitude toward outsiders, whom they characterized as "sons of darkness." John believed in encountering the world and calling people to conversion. He judged that people were sinners, but capable of salvation. He prepared them for the savior of the world.

John made the message of Isaiah live again in a new world. More vividly yet, he made his hero, Elijah, the model for his lifestyle. Like his beloved biblical mentor, John wore an itchy camel hide for a robe and dined ascetically on locusts and wild honey. He looked wretched. He adopted a way of life that challenged any observer. Yet crowds surged to the Jordan to hear his stern message of moral renewal and spiritual rebirth. Disciples joined him and followed his leadership.

The Baptist suited the spirit of the age. The restless people dreamed of a restoration of their ancient glory. They wanted freedom from all foreign domination. They yearned for another poet-warrior king like David to come and liberate them. The somber monastic community at Qumran believed there was so much sin and evil in the world that all of it had to come to an end. But a new world would be born again with them. Their "Teacher of Righteousness" would come and make it happen. They expected his arrival at any moment.

Like the superb teacher that he was, John capitalized on the mood of his listeners. He knew the pulse of the people and touched it. Were they expecting a new David? Were they hoping for a Teacher of Righteousness? So much the better. They wanted some kind of savior. They were wrong about the kind they sought. The elite at Qumran looked in the wrong place. The eager crowd at the Jordan mixed nostalgia with discontent and came to a false conclusion.

They should really have expected a spiritual messiah. John did not leave them in doubt. The real Messiah will come soon in fire and the Holy Spirit. The rushing enthusiasm of Elijah filled his words and unceremoniously confronted the listeners with a message much more dynamic than the temporizing they hoped to hear. No flight from the world will work, such as that practiced at Qumran. No armed militancy, advocated by the crowd, has much of a future. Neither fight nor flight prepared anyone for the arrival of the savior. Only moral conversion would work. Repentance would open their hearts to the spiritual rebirth that would be given by the true savior.

Many people waded into the waters, knelt before John, confessed aloud their sins, and received his baptism. Many refused. John preached that God's purifying fire had come, as predicted by the last prophet, Malachi (cf. 3:1). If one had the stuff of gold ore, God's fire would make a person shine with golden hope. If one were committed to be a straw in the wind, the divine fire would confirm the person's decision to be ashes borne away in the breeze.

John exhorted the people to prepare for the savior. Then Jesus came.

If John is the master of ceremonies, Christ is the guest of honor. The text records no familial greetings between the cousins. No hugs described or family news reported. This was a spiritual summit meeting and divine business must be addressed without distracting pleasantries. Joshua had ushered Israel into the promised land. Now Jesus/Yeshua would lead all people into the ultimate promised land of God's kingdom.

Jesus knelt in the water but did not confess any sins, for there were none to tell. He adopted the posture of a sinner out of sympathy and compassion to let all sinners know he loved them and would liberate them from humanity's worst problem, the problem of sin. He accepted the cleansing sign to show this would be his own mission.

As Jordan's baptismal waters flowed over the body of Jesus, the sky opened and revealed the mystery of God's dwelling place. God the Father spoke to Jesus words of love and pleasure. "You are my beloved Son; with you I am well pleased" (verse 11).

The Holy Spirit, dove-like, rested over him. In the creation story of Genesis, God's breath-like spirit hovered over the chaotic waters and from it drew the dawn of a new world. "Darkness covered the abyss, while a mighty wind swept over the waters" (Gn. 1:2). Now over the waters of the Jordan, the Spirit hovers to confirm the dawn of a new creation in Christ.

Immediately, the Spirit "drove" (verse 12) Jesus to the nearby desert for a confrontation with evil. Mark does not describe the details of the temptations found in the other gospels. Jesus here will struggle with the "wild beasts" who symbolize the forces of evil that Jesus must conquer. Neither his divine sonship nor his masterful human nature will immunize him from the unsettling assaults of temptation to evil.

Israel had spent forty years in the desert struggling against the temptations to go back to the flesh pots of Egypt and to give up the covenant God had struck with them. Christ's forty days in the desert recall that battle. They proclaim the beginning of his many victories over Satan and forecast his ultimate victory over sin and death in the triumph at the Cross and in the Resurrection. The ministering angels that will announce Easter already appear to celebrate Christ's first major conquest of evil.

The scenes of the baptism and the temptation introduce a divine and supernatural presence to the everyday details that preceded them. Heavens open. The Spirit descends. The Father speaks. Satan tempts. Angels minister. God has not left the world alone to fend for itself. Jesus Christ, Messiah, Son of Man, and Son of God has come to lavish love, affection, and forgiveness on every human being.

Christ Speaks and Acts with Authority (Mk. 1:14-45)

Jesus grew up in Galilee. It was the natural starting point for his ministry, which he began after his baptism and desert temptation. He knew the people and understood their hopes and fears. He heard them speak many times about their annoyance with their southern brethren in Judea who considered them second class Jews. Behind this superior attitude lay a story of the erosion of covenant faith among one group and a fierce adherence to it by another.

After Solomon's death (922 B.C.), civil war resulted in the division of his empire. The northern kingdom contained Samaria and

Galilee. The southern kingdom became Judea. Subsequent conquests of the northern kingdom by Babylon (722 B.C.) and other powers caused a decline of faith in Samaria and its virtual disappearance in Galilee. So many families from other countries and religions moved in that Galilee became known as "Galilee of the gentiles."

In Judea, however, the Jewish exiles who came back from Babylon brought with them a strict, almost puritan, Judaism which they developed to protect the covenant faith and memory. They rebuilt the temple and submitted themselves to a host of laws and practices meant to assure the safety and security of their religion.

About a century before Christ's birth, the Jewish Hasmonean kings invaded Galilee and forcibly converted the inhabitants to Judaism. Resettlement of Jewish families from Judea up to Galilee consolidated this move. The Judeans, however, judged that the plan never worked as well as it should have. They concluded that the Galileans were an inferior form of Judaism. Since Jesus belonged to the Judean family of David, however, the slight did not apply to him.

On the other hand, Jesus loved his "second class" Galileans. His ministry among them would be the happiest part of his mission. And it was from them he chose the apostles. Normally, students sought out a rabbi and asked to be his disciples. Jesus reversed this custom and searched for and chose his disciples.

He started by picking two sets of brothers, Peter and Andrew, James and John. He found them at the Galilean lakeshore tending their fishing boats. The historian Josephus reported that, in his day, 330 fishing boats sailed the lake. Jesus selected his first apostles from a major industry of his time and place. These men owned nets and had employees. From a human point of view, they unaccountably abandoned a secure and thriving business. They could probably read and write and had a general knowledge of the Bible.

Jesus simply called them to follow him and they did. The gospel does not portray him as using preparation or persuasion to convince them. Nor does the text comment on their possible resistance, either due to the impracticality of leaving the family business or some inner doubt about the credibility of Jesus. Far from being a process of anguished decision making, it is a quick and clean encounter. Jesus calls. They respond. Love attracted love.

The first act of preaching and healing ministry occurs at the

Capernaum synagogue which bordered the lake of Galilee. The congregation sat on benches that lined three of the walls or sat on the stone floor. The fourth wall faced Jerusalem. Soft candlelight glowed from the seven branched lamp near a lectern on a raised platform.

Jesus served as prayer leader that morning. The leader need not be a priest, nor the synagogue official who supervised the service and blew powerful blasts on the ram's horn to announce a sabbath service. Any adult male member could lead the prayer. Christ's voice rang out with thanks and praise to God for the blessings of the patriarchs and thanked the God who would bring them a savior and true peace.

The people shouted an Amen! Together, they recited their holiest prayer, the Shema. "Hear, 0 Israel! The Lord is our God. The Lord alone!" (Dt. 6:4). The synagogue administrator brought forward the wooden chest that contained the scrolls of the Torah, the first five books of the Bible. Unfolding one of the scrolls, he held it up for all to see. Then he laid it on the reading desk. Jesus invited a reader to recite a passage, after which a prayer of gratitude was said.

Then Jesus gave them a teaching. He amazed them because he spoke on his own authority, that is, he did not quote a lot of other authorities as was customary. He locked in their attention as he explained the Scripture. The Word of God explained the Word of God.

Then a scream pierced the intense quiet of that seaside synagogue. It came from a man possessed by an unclean spirit. With the same commanding authority he used to illumine the Scripture, Jesus said, "Quiet! Come out of him" (verse 25). The spirit convulsed the man and left him. Jesus again amazed them. Not only does he have authority to interpret the Scripture, he even has authority over unclean spirits. He needs no rituals, gestures nor magical tricks. He simply uses his commanding voice and personal authority.

After the service he went to the home of Simon and Andrew. Simon's mother-in-law was sick in bed with a fever. Jesus grasped her hand and helped her up. The fever left her and she offered them hospitality. The eventful day concludes with evening healings. Jesus had healed a man in the synagogue, a woman in Simon's home and now proceeds to heal a multitude in the street in front of Simon's home. Human suffering streams to him on foot, on the shoulders of the strong, on stretchers carried by the hopeful. Jesus welcomes them all into his heart and makes them new again. In the exorcisms of unclean spirits, the demons shout that they know Christ's real identity. Jesus quiets them because only his death on the cross will truly reveal who he is.

The miracles excited the people and generated false hopes in them. They marveled at his authoritative teaching style. His miracles astonished them. Such a man should also have power against political oppression. He could organize them. Power fantasies danced in their heads. They would never quite understand that Jesus' primary mission was to save them from the oppression of sin. If that led to other kinds of liberation, fine, but that was not his immediate goal.

His busy day in Capernaum had stirred up passions in people that needed cooling. Jesus quietly stole away to a deserted place and prayed. He gathered up his whole person and turned himself to communion with God. This refreshed and renewed him even as it braked the unhealthy enthusiasm of the crowds. It also focused his principal mission. "Let us go on to the nearby villages that I might preach there also. For this purpose have I come" (verse 38).

In another town a leper came to him and asked for a cure. Jesus does not recoil from the man. Whatever fears or anxieties the leper might have aroused in Jesus, they are not strong enough to turn Jesus away from him. Jesus stands his ground in the face of this profound human suffering. Moved by the deepest compassion for this man who was the poorest of all the poor, Jesus embraced the untouchable, said the words of healing, and cured him. He ordered the man to go to the priest who will verify the healing. Leviticus 14 describes the process for this act.

Thus a tide of human suffering washed up against Jesus at the very beginning of his ministry. Jesus did not avoid it or try to control it. He faced it resolutely with the tenderness of a nurse and the determined healing intention of a doctor. His loving heart is stronger than any pain that is brought to him.

Jesus goes with the flow of pain, meeting it as it comes to him. His healing acts are more than a ministry of service. He probes deeper to the very connection between sin, estrangement from God, and the existence of human suffering. Jesus does more than cure symptoms. He wants to heal the ultimate causes of human misery, to set things right again, to reconcile all that has been divided by sin.

Jesus is more than a human healer, loosening frozen limbs and opening up ears and eyes. Jesus touches, speaks, looks, and walks with the power of the Spirit flowing through him. Underneath the pleasures of the grateful eyes of those who are healed, lies the presence of divine healing. Jesus brings us back to bone and soul and heart, to the pillars of being human which are sustained by divine power and healing. He says it himself, as clearly as a bell. "For this purpose have I come" (verse 38).

Reflection

1. Do I hunger to meet a person who will witness God to me? Have I met someone like that?
2. Do I believe there are prophets in the world today? If so, who are they? Why are they considered prophets?
3. John the Baptist concluded that flight from the world or fighting the powers that be are not sufficient ways to prepare to receive Christ our Savior. What is the best way?
4. What does my baptism mean for me? What mission does baptism call me to? Am I responding?
5. Do I appreciate that Jesus really experienced temptations? How do I cope with the temptations in my life?
6. Jesus chose his disciples. They did not pick him. Have I understood that Christ has chosen me? How am I responding?
7. Christ spoke with a personal authority strengthened by his witness. Is my Christian witness strong enough to make my words credible?
8. Jesus took time for prayer. Do I save time each day for prayer?
9. Jesus readily healed all kinds of pain. Am I open and compassionate toward the hurts and pain of others?
10. Jesus healed the deeper problem, that of sin. Am I open to a lifelong conversion from sin to grace and goodness?

Prayer

Jesus, fulfiller of the dreams of all the prophets, you healed others by your words and deeds. You move us to see the divine healer behind these miracles and ask us to see the ultimate healing from sin. Heal me. Forgive me. Renew me. Make me whole again.

2 From a Rooftop to a Cornfield

Healing the Soul and the Body (Mk. 2:1-12)

Many people say, "I can forgive others. I have a hard time forgiving myself." Unfortunately, some people cannot forgive others either. But the fact remains that a majority of people know they need forgiveness. Some know how to seek it. Some fumble all their lives with the problem of guilt and sin. Occasionally, forgiveness floods a life unexpectedly as in Christ's healing of the paralytic.

It all began on a rooftop. Jesus had returned to Capernaum and was delivering the Gospel to an overflow crowd in Simon's home. Excavations of fishermen's houses in Capernaum show us a picture of stone dwellings. Plaster coated the outside walls. A roof of reeds and sticks packed with thick clay kept out the rain. Grass often grew from the earth pack on the roof.

Opening a hole in such a roof was an easy matter. Also, repairing it was relatively simple. Four men, carrying a paralytic, climbed the stairway that led to the roof. They dug a hole in it and let their friend down into the room where Jesus was preaching. This room was used for living and dining. At night the family slept on the floor on straw mats.

Christian imagination has added details to this story. In one version, the four men are sons carrying their stricken father, with a worried wife in attendance. A strange disease had suddenly assaulted the man. Without warning his body stiffened into paralysis. No doctor knew what to do. The family feared he would die soon. They heard that Jesus could heal. The crowd would not let them in the door. What else could they do? Desperately, they settled for opening the roof and lowering the sick man on ropes right down to the floor in front of Jesus.

Jesus looked down on the man in front of him. He gazed up at the woman and her four sons staring at him with hope and faith.

Simon was not amused to see his roof with a gaping hole in it. He had yelled loudly and futilely for them to stop. On the other hand, Jesus felt the joy of their faith and loved the daring way they chose to express it. Simon scowled. Jesus smiled. Jesus took the man's hand and felt the stiffness in his arms. He stroked the man's forehead to calm him and give him some reassurance in this very public and strange setting.

The room grew very still. In silent excitement they awaited a miracle. Several of those present had witnessed Christ's earlier cures. The rest had never seen a real miracle. They waited with a mixture of awe and plain curiosity.

Jesus surprised and disappointed them.

With a solemn directness, Jesus said to the paralyzed man, "My son, your sins are forgiven" (verse 6).

Christ's peace flowed like a river into the paralytic whose faced reflected gratitude for a long sought gift. Immobilized on his bed, he had spent long hours reviewing his life. Raised in a culture and a religion that taught a connection between sin and sickness, he looked long and hard at his moral life. Basically, he judged himself to have been a good man, a devoted husband, and a responsible father. Slowly, however, his moral failures surfaced.

A little dishonesty here, a small lie there, a forgetfulness of his wife's needs and his sons' training, an accumulation of minor injustices and failures to love, a neglect of his social responsibilities — this may not have added up to a dark and evil portrait, but it was a flawed one. Gradually, he honestly faced his sinfulness, not so much one that left behind a list of broken moral laws, more one that broke the fit between him and God. The more he began to think about the holy purity of God, the closer he came to an honest appreciation of himself. The nearer he drew to God, the more he felt far from God.

Then this wonderful and unexpected gift touched his heart. He was carried to the feet of Jesus. Everything felt right in the presence of Jesus. He understood that Jesus was supposed to cure him. He was human enough to want to get up and walk like other people. But his meditations had released a hunger for freedom from another kind of bondage, the deeply rooted sinfulness he now understood.

But while others waited for a miracle, the paralytic enjoyed communion with Jesus. Walls dropped. He was ready for the best of all miracles, the forgiveness of sins. Jesus did not disappoint him. His words spoke forgiveness. His words produced it, snapping the chain that prevented the reconciliation, the experience of rightness so long desired. The others may have felt let down. He felt a satisfaction so sublime nothing else mattered.

Into that spiritual reverie a discordant note broke the spell. Some religious scholars inwardly condemned the act as blasphemy. Superficially, they are right. Only God could forgive sin. Jesus could perform all the miracles he wished. After all, had not great prophets done the same? But he was wrong to pronounce forgiveness of sins.

Jesus saw the displeasure on their faces and understood their objection. He tried to lead them to see what had happened. They believed in the link between sickness and sin. Literally, if sin is forgiven then a sickness could disappear. Jesus asks whether it is easier to forgive a sin or cure a body. They look at him blankly. Jesus followed through by referring to himself as the Son of Man who has authority on earth to forgive sins. To prove this he said to the paralytic, "I command you. Stand up! Pick up your mat and go home" (verse 11).

Healed in soul and body, the man unfolded his frozen limbs and stood up to the roar of his family and the people who praised God for the physical healing, not the spiritual one. That, for the moment, remained a private secret between Jesus and the cured man. With a parting look of gracious thanks, the man joined his family and departed.

The scholars now had a dilemma to face. They could see the cure. They could not see the forgiveness. Yet by their religious theory it had to have happened. Still, this did not convince them. It was too new, too bizarre, not worthy of being believed, but certainly an upsetting turn of events. Instead of awakening in them a sense of wonder, the event closed them up in their traditions. Their accusation of blasphemy would be heard again at Christ's trial before the religious court. They would join an increasing band of opposition to Jesus. Christ's conflict with the powers that would destroy him began at this hour. The first cloud appeared on the sunny horizon of the Galilean ministry.

Sick People Need Doctors (Mk. 2:13-17)

Up to this point Jesus had walked a careful path, cheerfully healing people and selecting solid, respected citizens for his disciples. He shook up a few scribes, but made everybody else feel good about his message and mission. He possessed that kind of popularity that comes from having done nothing as yet to offend the self-congratulatory feelings of those who knew and followed him. He had given them the soothing milk, suitable for children. It was time now to give them the solid food of adults. Saint Paul was to follow the same pattern. "I fed you milk, not solid food, because you were unable to take it. . . Yet we do speak a wisdom to those who are mature" (I Cor. 3:2; 2:6).

Jesus had chosen four pillars of the lakeshore fishing industry for his first apostles. Popular selections all, these men reinforced a positive attitude toward the new rabbi who was becoming a celebrity. Then the other shoe fell. Jesus shocked them all by picking Levi, the despised tax collector for Capernaum as his fifth apostle. As a sign of his conversion, Levi, son of Alphaeus, would have his name changed to Matthew. Jesus risked the turmoil that inevitably followed. It was a gamble that had to be taken, for his message was deeper than a simple stroking of the complacent respectability of the local culture.

The kingdom would include more than loveable and admired community leaders. It would even embrace the man they all loved to hate. Levi was a non-practicing Jew. The Romans had hired him to collect the taxes. In the deal that was struck, Levi was expected to turn over so much money per family to the imperial treasury. He would exact more money than that and keep the difference. Everyone knew the system and they all hated it and despised the collaborator who made it possible.

Probably none were more upset that the two sets of brothers Jesus had enlisted as his first apostles. Their fishing profits would have been a special target for Levi. One could easily hear Peter shouting at Jesus, "How could you want that bloodsucker, my worst enemy, as a member of our inner circle? Are you crazy?"

Far from backing down, Jesus upped the ante. He went to Matthew's home for a dinner party. Naturally, Matthew invited his circle of friends, other tax collectors and their families as well as additional moral outcasts of Galilean society. He violated the customary law of the table. It was not God's law, but it was so ingrained in the religious culture of the people that it bore — incorrectly — the stamp of divine approval.

That law decreed that Jewish families, which kept the Law of Moses, should not fraternize with those that disobeyed it. Above all this meant never entering such peoples' homes, and certainly never eating at table with them. To break bread and drink wine with them would be tantamount to approving their sinful lifestyle. The tax collectors and sinners were considered unclean. Contact with them meant becoming morally stained oneself.

The news spread throughout the town that Jesus was enjoying himself at Matthew's banquet. In that warm climate, doors were left open and curiosity seekers could pause by the door, look in and see what was happening. Mark notes that some scribes who were Pharisees came to check on the truth of the rumor. Very likely, the first four apostles lingered — and smoldered — at the door as well. Stunned and dismayed, they all said, "Why does he eat with tax collectors and sinners?" Jesus had brought them all to the teachable moment. It was time for solid food. Milk was for children. They must grow up and appreciate the deeper demands of his message. Those who are well do not need a physician, but the sick do. I did not come to call the righteous, but sinners (Mk. 2:17).

To their credit, the four apostles were willing to stretch themselves morally and spiritually. They did accept Matthew as a comrade. It doubtless helped them that Matthew left his lucrative business at the tax house and clearly was willing to change his ways. The "good" apostles gradually learned another lesson. They were sinners too and needed the ministrations of Jesus their doctor.

Should I Fast? Should I Eat? (Mk. 2:18-22)

Up to this point Mark states that Jesus taught with authority. Now Mark reveals the content of Christ's teachings. In that very sociable society of the biblical mideast where conversation — with its story telling, gossip, debates, and dialogues — was daily entertainment, a teacher would get across his message in just such a setting.

Jesus skillfully used these settings to share his good news. The topic of fasting arose. Someone asked Jesus why he and his disciples had no fasting rules. The followers of the baptist were famed for their ascetical fasting lifestyle. The pharisees and their followers fasted twice a week. It was easy to tell who they were, for they whitened their faces and mussed up their clothes on Mondays and Thursdays (their fast days) to prove it. Every Jew was expected to fast only once a year on the day of Atonement. Does Jesus approve of fasting? If so, why does he not impose some rules of fasting on his people?

Jesus obviously had no problem with the value of fasting. Had he not begun his ministry with forty days of fasting in the desert? He took up their fasting question to highlight an attitude he expected of his followers. He reminded them of the happiest days in the life of any Jew, namely, the seven days of a wedding feast. No one should fast that week. The guests are expected to enjoy themselves.

By contrast, Jesus implies that fasters not only deny themselves enjoyment of food, but often become miserable and shed their discontent on others with their sad faces and moods. They forget that fasting is a means to an end, namely, inner peace and the joy that should follow.

Jesus says that being with him is like being at a wedding. That is why his followers do not fast. Because of communion with him, they have acquired the habit of joy which fasting is supposed to bring about. Fasting is meant to purify the person from morose behavior and attitudes and release the joy that God has planted deep within each person's heart.

After he is gone, historically, Christians will fast because they need to struggle to get in touch with him in his risen presence through the Spirit. But the purpose will be the same, to acquire a habit of joy. He, the bridegroom, will be present in the church and in the sacraments and in the loving community of the redeemed. Fasting will be one means of uniting with him, the cause of their joy.

Jesus asks them to realize the utter newness of his approach. They must shed old categories. None of them would put a new patch on an old and useless garment, for it would tear away. None of them would put new wine in old wineskins, because the old, stiff wineskin would crack open, being unable to contain the volatile and vigorous new wine. Their mindsets require new clothes, not patches, new wineskins, not the brittle old ones. He will expect Christians to be joyful. Some day they may have to fast to acquire this habit of the heart.

Hungry Disciples and Irritated Pharisees (Mk. 2:23-28)

On the following sabbath, Jesus and his disciples were walking through a cornfield. The hungry comrades picked a few ears of corn and chewed on them. Probably the owner of the field saw them and reported the incident to the Pharisees, who thereupon accused the disciples of breaking the law against working on the sabbath. In any other context, common sense would never have judged so trivial an act as working. Picking and nibbling on a few ears of corn requires so little effort that it takes a lot of imagination to think of it as work.

Not so, however, in that tight little religious culture of long ago. What began as a good thing during their exile in Babylon grew into a monster with the passing years. Jewish religious leaders and prophets had seen how easy it had been to break a love relationship (a covenant) with God and its painful results in exile. They were desperate and determined to see that this would not happen again. Hence on top of the biblical list of laws, they added numerous customs to dictate every aspect of life. With the passing years such laws encrusted the holy core of revealed divine law in the Torah (the first five books of the Bible). The law of unintended consequences took over. What was meant to free people for a covenant love affair with God, locked them up instead under a heavy burden of senseless laws and customs.

Jesus understood the problem perfectly and had come to liberate people not only from their sins, but also from religious absurdities that choked off their good natures and robbed them of their common sense. The Pharisees had challenged him with a question. In a very mideastern manner, he replied with a question that reminded them of a scriptural story that illustrated that honest human need is superior to a law. He goes even further to enunciate a principle that law is meant to serve the spiritual and physical needs of humans as they try to stay in touch with God's love. "The sabbath was made for man, not man for the sabbath" (verse 27).

Chapter 2 of Mark has introduced the first jolts in an otherwise ideal and serene Galilean ministry. Three conflict stories demonstrate how Christ's message and ministry would lead to a painful conclusion in Holy Week. Scribes worry about what they perceive as Christ's daring and blasphemous absolution of the sins of the paralytic. Pharisees are appalled that Jesus chooses a hated tax collector as a disciple and breaks the law of table fellowship by eating with sinners and tax collectors, the pariahs of the community. Again the Pharisees are upset by the breaking of the sabbath law about work.

They see that Jesus is no easy-going fashionable preacher, nursing the self congratulatory myths of the successful and respectable locals. He is much more like the prophets of old who upset the accepted order. He even seems like a false prophet to them. In any case he is dangerous. They must watch and curb him.

Reflection

1. If I were the paralytic, would I have been disappointed to hear that Jesus forgave my sins and, as yet, said nothing about curing me?
2. The friends of the paralytic dug a hole in the roof to let their friend down into Jesus' presence. In modern terms, would I consider that a case of illegal "breaking and entering?"
3. How would I have answered Jesus' question — Is it easier to forgive sins or to heal a paralytic? Is forgiveness really easy?
4. Who are the tax collectors in my little world? What families would I "not be found dead" with?
5. Do I sympathize with the first four apostles' dismay at Jesus' choice of Matthew? How would I have felt?
6. Am I a person who is forever going on another diet? At the same time, do I see any value in fasting for religious reasons?
7. Am I a sad Christian, or a joyful one?
8. Do I think there are religious laws today that lack common sense?
9. Do I understand that the commandments are laws to help us to love God, self, and others? Or do I see them as restrictive commands?
10. Has our culture gone too far in secularizing the sabbath?

Prayer

Jesus, Lord of life, you have fed us with the milk we needed to start on our journey of faith. You command us to grow up, however, and partake of the solid food of maturing. Make us ready and willing to march on. Open us up to a future with hope and courage.

3   Christ's Emotions and a Family Crisis

He Looked at Them With Anger (Mk. 3:1-12)

Did Jesus have emotions? Did he have feelings? The questions tend to generate quick "Of course he did — Of course he didn't" reactions. Those who over-idealize Jesus, wanting him to be so masterful that his feet barely touch the earth, will nervously explain away any gospel language about Christ's emotional life. Those who argue strenuously for the reality of his humanity, forcefully defend his having emotions but grow hesitant when anyone speaks about his creative mastery of his life of feelings.

Ask Mark this question and he replies with a forthright yes. Here is a catalog of Christ's feelings in Mark:

— He was moved with pity, 1:45
— Jesus, warning him sternly, 1:43
— He groaned, 7:34
— He sighed, 8:12
— He became indignant, 10:14
— Jesus, looking at him, loved him, 10:21

A truly human Jesus feels, emotes. A genuinely integrated Jesus puts his feelings at the service of his mission of salvation. He does more than control his feelings, he harmonizes them with his mind, his soul and his mysterious union with divine Love.

An example of this occurs in his return to the Capernaum synagogue. At his first visit he exorcised an unclean spirit from an unfortunate man at the services. That was the springtime of his Galilean ministry. Since then, however, a series of conflicts with religious leaders has introduced tension between him and them. At this religious gathering they sit there, not with pleasant faces enjoying the sweet pleasure of watching another wonder worker plying his trade, but with searching, judgmental eyes.

They have become suspicious list makers of his affronts to traditional laws and customs. This is a sabbath day. They wait to see if he will heal on the sabbath, an act contrary to their laws about sabbath work. Only saving someone from death is allowed.

Once again the synagogue rituals unfold — Jesus prays, the administrator brings the scrolls, someone reads — and now it is time for Jesus' sermon. Only now Jesus changes the usual procedure. He asks a man with a withered hand to come forward. He takes the man's lifeless hand and enfolds it tenderly in his own hands. Cradling that wrinkled hand, Jesus asks the experts whether it is permitted to do a good deed on the sabbath or an evil one, to save life or destroy it.

They said nothing. He had exposed the foolishness of their rules. They had made the holiest day of the week one in which doing a good deed was forbidden. Perversely, it also became a day when evil occurred because of laws causing the omission of a good act.

Their silence angered him. Their insensitivity to human sorrow grieved him. "Looking around at them with anger and grieved at their hardness of heart" (verse 5), Jesus, clearly, could have had an emotional reaction to an event that deserved it. God is love. The very representatives of God used a religious law to block the giving of love. They closed their minds to Jesus, the embodiment of love. They preferred the presumed sanctity of a rule to the healing of a person. God's rules were meant to be windows of love, means to affection, not methods for control or obstacles to good work.

Still, Jesus does not wallow in emotion for its own sake. Emotion is a motivator. Emotion — as its Latin origin implies — moves. It can move one to good or evil. In Christ's case, feelings always move him to doing the good for which he came. Jesus sanctifies the life of the emotions. He released the man's hand and asked him to stretch it out for all to see. No word was spoken. The silence of hate from the religious leaders was matched by Christ's creative silence. As they all watched, the hand came to life, the skin glowed and the movement returned.

Now it was the Pharisees turn to have their moment of aroused emotions, but their feelings moved them to destructive behavior. In a biblical application of the motto, "Politics makes strange bedfellows," they allied themselves with the Herodians against Jesus. The Pharisees who would plot the death of Jesus join up with the Herodians who caused the death of John the Baptist.

The religious leaders hardened their hostility to Jesus, but the people still loved him. Not only did Jews come from all over to see and hear him and be cured, but also gentiles from Transjordan, Tyre, and Sidon. They surged toward him to touch him. The sorrow of the world flowed to his person. His love was flowing like a river, flowing out to Jews and gentiles alike, flowing out from him like the great waters of the lake where he showered them with his cures. The crush of the crowd became so great he ordered a boat so he could avoid their overwhelming him.

To Be Near Jesus — to Preach His Message (Mk. 3:13-19)

Jesus left the lake area and went to a mountain. On that quiet height, he took a major step in his mission. He must provide for the continuity of his message and work of salvation. He knew he would die. Someone must preach his message and do his work after he was gone. For that purpose he named twelve men to be his apostles. He expected them to be near him, to act as his heralds, and to cast out demons. Others might come and go. These were to stay in his company where he could write his message on their hearts, form them into disciples, and prepare them for their future ministry.

They sat around him on that mountaintop and heard him call each one of them by name. Isaiah had earlier taught that God loved to call people in a personal way. "Do not be afraid. I have redeemed you. I have called you by your name. You are mine because you are precious in my eyes, because I love you" (Is. 43:2,4). As a master of Scripture, Jesus may very well have used this text, since it applied so perfectly to this event.

Names are important in Scripture. The turning points of Scripture revolve around naming events. Quite easily, a person can say, "My name is me. My name is one of the sweetest sounds I know." God thinks so, too. God never gets mixed up about people's names. God does not call Lucy, Isabella. The Lord does not mistake Ed for

Bill. "Upon the palms of my hands I have written your name" (Is. 49:16).

At this turning point, Jesus looks at the twelve with love and calls them to their destiny, each one by name. Peter, who would have a bumpy journey of faith, was overly enthusiastic, fearful even to the point of denying Jesus, but was finally able to surrender in love. Andrew, his brother, about whom little will be known, though tradition claimed he died on a cross formed as an X. James and John are so fiery of temperament that they are called the sons of thunder. John would bank his emotional fires so that God, according to tradition, could turn him into a mystical-like disciple and the best writer about Christian love. Herod would kill James with a sword. Matthew had given up tax collecting and one day would write a gospel. Then there is Philip, a friend of Andrew and Peter. He would in turn introduce Nathaniel (other name, Bartholomew) to Jesus. Thomas would become the famous doubter — and fervent man of faith. After Thomas is James the Less, that is, the Younger, to distinguish him from John's brother. Then there is Jude, also known as Thaddeus. Following him is Simon the Zealot, formerly a nationalist (some might even say, terrorist), now committed to the peace of Christ. Sadly, at the end of the line is Judas, the man from Kerioth, who would betray Jesus.

Jesus looked at them all: a terrorist, a hated tax man, a doubter, a brace of temperamental brothers, a future mystic, denier, and a betrayer. Of such a gallery of human characters did he build his apostolic community. A practical person would call this madness. A comedian might frame it in terms of a divine sense of humor. Jesus looked at them with eyes of love and saw what love's magic would accomplish.

Jesus did not pick saints. He chose pilgrims. He would walk with them and talk with them. He expected them to stay near him and allow themselves to be transformed by his presence and his love. All of them responded except one. Not a bad average, indeed, better than most.

Christ's Family Worries About Him (Mk. 3:20-35)

Mark now introduces Christ's family into the narrative. Unlike Matthew and Luke, Mark does not recount the infancy stories. He begins with the adult Jesus arriving at the Jordan for his baptism.

What may be said about Christ's family? Given the fact that life spans in biblical times rarely exceeded the age of forty, one can assume that both sets of Christ's grandparents were deceased. Almost certainly, Christ's father, Joseph, has died. None of the gospels portray Joseph as alive or present in any active way during Christ's public ministry. Popular Catholic devotion has accepted this view, picturing Joseph dying in the arms of Jesus and Mary, thus becoming the patron of a happy death. Clearly, Christ's mother is alive and active at certain key moments such as the marriage feast of Cana and the crucifixion.

Jesus would have belonged to a typical mideastern extended family of those days. These are close-knit families, where bloodlines count and aunts, uncles and cousins mingle frequently, eat together often, supervise each other's children, tell each other gossip and stories for mutual bonding and entertainment, monitor family values and behavior, and lend an economic hand where needed.

Joseph and Mary were privileged to know Jesus from a faith perspective. To them he may have remained a mystery but he was no problem child or perplexing adult. But what did the other relatives think? Jesus must have been a puzzle to his extended family for many years. In a culture that expected sons and daughters to marry, Jesus chose to be celibate. Prior to his public ministry, his celibacy may have been the major discordant note he struck with his family.

Suddenly, he became a public figure, performing miracles, packing the synagogue with crowds eager to hear his sermons and attracting hordes of people for his healing ministry. So far so good. Most likely, the family took vicarious pride in the fame of their newly distinguished relative. He was popularly loved and admired.

Then shadows and clouds blocked out the sunny days. The family heard a series of distressing reports. A scribe called him a blasphemer for forgiving a sin. A committee of religious leaders threatened to take action against him for curing the man with the withered hand on a sabbath day — and in a synagogue at that. His choice of the community's most unpopular man, the tax collector, angered his family as much as anyone else. Their local tax collector at Nazareth had stung them just as much as others.

Some of the family's elders began to wonder about Christ's stability. Did he have brain sickness? Was he burnt out by his incessant activity? Did he shows signs of some nervous disorder? No question but that Jesus was embarrassing his family. The once envious neighbors now began to laugh at the family. The relatives decided they must bring Jesus home for a family council. He was affecting their inner peace and outward reputation.

When they found out he was at Peter's house, their worst suspicions were confirmed. A wall of people surrounded the house. So tightly were they packed in that it was impossible to bring food into the dwelling. In the family's eyes, the whole scene was a circus, a wild and uncontrollable force that convinced them they must take charge of Jesus. Seeing the bedlam, they concluded Jesus must be "out of his mind" (verse 21). They somehow sent word in they wanted to see him.

As Jesus emerged from the house, a delegation of scribes from Jerusalem stopped him. Obviously, the Galilean preacher and wonder-worker was too dangerous to be ignored by the highest officials of religion. The scribes confronted him with the blasphemy accusation, the revolt against the sabbath laws and his defiance of the law of table fellowship by his eating with sinners. He was openly threatening a careful, centuries-old system of rituals, customs, and laws designed to protect covenant life.

In their minds, only an evil person could act this way. They stared at him and judged that an evil spirit possessed him. Beelzebub, the prince of demons, controlled him. Jesus replied by showing how illogical was their judgment. Did it make any sense to say that the devil casts out the devil? That does not follow. Why should the devil give up control of a person? That would be like the devil declaring civil war on himself. It would be satanic suicide. If he did that his kingdom would collapse.

Then Jesus reminded them about the unforgivable sin, blasphemy against the Holy Spirit. An evil spirit did not act in him. The

Holy Spirit did. They were looking at good acts, that originated from God, and saying the devil did it. They should have discerned the Holy Spirit, but saw an unholy spirit instead. They have rejected love and refused the kingdom. They have committed the unforgivable sin. However, the possibility of forgiveness lies ahead for them, if they open their hearts to Jesus. They will need interior conversion to receive forgiveness.

The family watched Jesus handle the scribes with the skill of a wise man and the stern language of a prophet. It was an impressive performance. Jesus did not back away from his formidable and prestigious accusers. He was in command of the situation. They had called him a blasphemer. Jesus told them they were the real blasphemers. And they were in trouble unless they changed.

Nothing is said about the family reaction. Would their practical natures make them wish Jesus were more tactful with the powerful visitors from Jerusalem? Had he not stirred up enough trouble? Maybe they could talk some sense into him. Blocked by the crowd, they again send a messenger to tell him they wanted to see him. Upon hearing of their presence, Jesus proceeded to tell the people that his real mother, brother, and sister is the person who hears the word of God and keeps it. When the family heard his response, they were probably more convinced than ever they must influence him into a more moderate direction. From their point of view, they would fail in this mission.

What then of Mary, his mother? The faith of Mary, deepened by thirty years of prayer and personal contact with Jesus, moved her to cooperate with her son's mysterious and dangerous mission. The mother had long ago become the disciple of her son. Her many years of communion with him and her surrender to God engendered in her the trust in the divine process that now unfolded so vividly before her eyes. No one knows what she might have said to the relatives. Most certainly, she realized that only faith made any sense out of what was happening. Somehow, the family must one day come to see Jesus in faith and accept the gift of discipleship. Since the gospels intrude no further on family privacy, the outcome is left to the imagination and the providence of God.

Reflection

1. Have I ever doubted or worried about Christ having feelings and an emotional life?
2. Was Christ's emotional response to the scribes justified and appropriate?
3. Is there any difference between the way Jesus expressed his feelings and my way of doing it?
4. What is the difference, if any, between Christ's response to his feelings and my response to my own?
5. Christ called his apostles by name. At what point in my life did Jesus call me by name?
6. Do I ever think that someone in my family is getting out of hand and needs talking to, seeming to be out of his or her mind?
7. Is Christ's family's reaction to him predictable and understandable?
8. The scribes' judgement about Christ was obviously unreasonable, especially for men trained in religious thought and practice. What blinded them?
9. How can I be a "mother, sister, and brother" to Jesus?
10. How does Mary model discipleship for me?

Prayer

Wise Jesus, your ways will sometimes seem like madness to others and, yes, to me. Divine methods do not always seem sensible in human terms. Yet your ways are the true paths to joy and fulfillment. Make me wise so I can be your true disciple.

4   The Storyteller

The Story as a Challenge (Mk. 4:1-34)

Biblical society was an oral culture. They did have books, but not many of them because paper was expensive and books were written by hand. Some people could read and write but due to the scarcity of books and writing materials, most communication was oral. Popular, face to face communication generally consisted of discussion, debate, haggling — and almost always some form of storytelling. Oral cultures thrived on stories.

Frequently, these stories were condensed into brief, poetic wisdom sayings. An oral culture was very much at home with poetry. The poetic imagination was not the possession of professionals, though great poets often did emerge because the whole society was tuned into the power and value of poetic expression. Most of the prophets were poets. That accounts for the tremendous power their words evoked, since they used this most dynamic form of speech for their messages. Oral cultures preferred communication that embraced the totality of life, not just abstract ideas about it.

Biblical people valued the spoken word. It is true if it is said. A person's word was a bond. That is why no one would be surprised if God made the world by a word. "Then God said, 'Let there be light.' and there was light" (Gn. 1:3). People thought it perfectly correct that Jesus could cure a person simply by speaking a word of healing. The Hebrew term for word is *dabar*, and it means both the spoken word as well as the action the word may imply. Words were more than chit-chat. Words had power.

Modern society is a document culture. The paper trail symbolizes the importance of the written word. It is true if it is written. What is written remains. What is said flies away on the wings of the wind. The written word is solid. The spoken word is volatile. A document culture favors abstract statements over anecdotes. A story entertains. It does not inform, teach, or instruct as well as abstract statements do. This is the bias of a document culture.

Abstraction implies serious business, rational competence, and the ability to master a topic and control a process. The more impersonal a written statement (the more objective it is), the more likely it is considered to be true. A story is too personal, too cluttered, too messy to be the vehicle for serious discussion. At best, it is comic relief. At worst, it is an interruption in the solemn flow of abstractly stated reports, professional opinions, and learned analyses.

The triumph of document culture imperils the appreciation of the biblical narrative, an enormous part of which is storytelling, poetry, and letter writing. It further obscures the power of that quintessential form of New Testament storytelling, the parables of Jesus. Modern education, with its emphasis on the rational — admittedly bringing huge positive benefits to society — has paid the price of suppressing skills buried in human consciousness, especially the power of imagining.

True, imagination survives in novels, films, TV dramas, and the texts of songs (probably the last trace of popular poetry available). But such use of imagination is performed by a few for the entertainment of the many. Its commercialization further diminishes its genuine identification with the human heart for the most part. These products of a document culture ape the human communion of an oral culture, but often fail because they restrain the imagination of the reader, viewer, and listener who receives, but seldom reacts or finds his or her imagination stirred up to respond.

Or if there is a reaction, it tends to be private and rarely an interpersonal one with the author or producer. Hence, even where imagination is active in modern society, it is a one way street performed by professional imaginers, resulting in yet another depreciation of the gift of human imagination in the receivers. Small wonder that someone has said that most novels, films, and TV dramas are little more than chewing gum for the eyes.

This comparison of oral and document cultures may shed some light when confronted with the parables of Jesus. His parables were more than stories with a moral, or stories with a doctrinal point to make. They were revelations of God's action in human affairs. They were stories of God acting on them right there in Galilee. They were moments of recognition and challenge for the hearers. They were more than entertainment. They were meant to be occasions for personal conversion.

Perhaps a modern clue can be found in the spellbinding storytelling of Garrison Keillor when he was broadcasting his Prairie Home Companion. The fact that he did it on radio emphasized the importance of listening. Moreover, the hearers needed to supply the context. The listeners had to use their imaginations. This not only increased their enjoyment but gave them the pleasure of a series of "wake-up" experiences that helped them to see their own lives in a fresh and welcoming way. This is about as close as we have come in a modern society to the oral culture of biblical days.

Which brings us to Christ's parables in Mark. Jesus is still enormously loved by ordinary people, though he is under suspicion in other quarters. This time, it is not his miracles that draw the people, but his teachings. So great is the attendance that Jesus boards a boat to escape their crush. He uses the boat as his pulpit. Some days before he had also escaped to a boat when those seeking a cure threatened to mob him. Both his saving deeds and his saving words possessed magnetic force.

In using parables, he not only followed the expectations of people in an oral culture, he placed himself in line with the storytellers of the Old Testament. The prophet Nathan had used a parable to wake up the conscience of King David who had let his lust for Bathsheba seduce her into betraying her husband, Uriah. It also led David to ordering the conditions which resulted in the death of Uriah in battle. Nathan's parable successfully called David to honest confession and conversion (cf. II Sm. 12:1-7).

Even to this day, rabbis often use parables. Here is one that has a humorous slant to it while it gently implants some wisdom in the listener. In a certain synagogue, two rabbis had died in swift succession. The new rabbi came into a situation where there was a dispute about whether to sit or stand during the Shema, their holiest prayer. His predecessor had insisted the people sit. The one before him argued the people should stand. The new rabbi went to the congregation's oldest member to find out what was the custom in his early years. Because of age, the man's memory was not as clear as one would like. He tried so hard to remember. The frustrated young rabbi said, "But you must try to recall what happened. The people are throwing prayer books at each other." A light flashed in his friend's eyes. "Yes! Yes! That's how it was." In some ways, nothing is new under the sun, for Christians could easily tell the same story about themselves.

Jesus taught the people with parables. Quite possibly, in this case he might have seen a farmer planting a field on the hillside near the lake. In which case he would have a ready visual image for his story. He could start with their human experience and offer them a revelation of God acting in their midst. His preliminary words would be, "Take a look at that farmer on the hill."

Then he would begin with the story of a farmer sowing his seed and the varying success of the farmer's efforts. From the time they were children, all his listeners would have seen how farmers sowed seed. The average plot of land of a Galilean farmer was about seven acres. He identified it by placing a pile of rocks around the perimeter.

He usually planted his wheat or barley seeds in the autumn after the hot summer winds died down and the moist air brought by the west winds from the sea had come, bringing the first rains since April. The rain softened the hard sun-baked fields, allowing the farmer the opportunity to plow his acreage. His plow was a wooden, V-shaped digging instrument with an iron tip at the bottom.

The farmer attached it to oxen or donkeys by means of leather or rope. He walked behind the animals, guiding the plow and prodding them with a goad (a sharp-edged metal instrument) as they pulled the plow and loosened the earth. He created furrows in one direction, then took a basket of seed and, with his hand, spread it in a waving, rhythmic motion over the new turned earth. Then he plowed the land again crosswise, covering the seed to keep the birds from eating it or the winds from blowing it away.

Jesus described the fate of the seeds. Birds would eat the seeds that were not plowed under. Seeds that landed on rock would wither and die. Thorns would choke other seeds. The seeds that fell on good soil would yield thirty- and sixty- and a hundredfold. A farmer considered himself lucky if he gained five bushels of grain from one bushel of seed. That is what fivefold means. When Jesus was to speak of a harvest that yielded a hundredfold, one can get a better idea of the impact on farmers who never even dreamed of reaping a tenfold harvest.

Up to this point Christ's parable described what any farmer knew, except the ending of his story. The extraordinary harvest of which Jesus spoke introduced a puzzling and impossible conclusion. The apostles asked Jesus about the parable. Jesus replied that his parables are calls to faith. Heard and received in faith, the parable becomes a revelation of God's invitation to the listener, calling for a conversion and behavioral response. Heard and received with rejection by others, the parable will point to their loss of the kingdom of God. Heard and received simply in human terms the parable remains a riddle to those listeners.

Jesus then proceeded to interpret the parable in terms of varying responses to God's call to conversion. The seed is God's word offering love, salvation, and forgiveness. People respond in different ways. Those on the foot path are people who have no interest in God's love. In a way they are the happy hedonists, much like the young California couple who said, "We surf on Sunday morning, ski in the afternoon, and dance at night. Religion can't compete with this."

Those on rocky ground are drifters. They float from one enthusiasm to another. Laid back and loose, they glide from belief to belief and from church to church. They get excited about God and then lose their fire. They are perpetual modern nomads in a rootless culture. If they experience persecution or opposition to their lifestyles, they give up altogether.

Those sown among thorns are the secularists, who might have had some religious fervor, but the craving for money and possessions overwhelms them and they settle for a materialistic lifestyle.

Those on good ground hear the word of God and keep it. They embark on the journey of faith and accept the demands of discipleship. They take God into their hearts and let the power of the Lord convert them. They will enjoy a harvest of thirty- and sixty- and a hundredfold.

It must be remembered that Jesus is doing more than describing a process. His parable challenges his listeners right then and there. He is evangelizing them and calling them to salvation. He is doing more than describing a process, he is involving them in one. He is inviting them to be loved and forgiven. This is not a lamp to be put under a bed, but on a stand to light people to the path of hope. This is a seed he expects to develop in the hearts of his hearers, a seed that mysteriously grows from blade to ear, to the ripe wheat. It may begin as small as a mustard seed, but one day it shall blossom into a tree so large that birds may dwell in its branches. Hence the journey of faith leads both to personal growth in holiness and a membership in the community of the redeemed. Thus has Jesus taken a simple rural image and turned it into a dramatic and profound invitation to a union with ultimate Love.

Who Is This Man? Even the Winds and Seas Obey Him (Mk. 4:35-41)

When the session on parables was finished, Jesus directed his apostles to take the boat to the opposite shore. Winds, coming over the hills west of the Sea of Galilee, swept down onto the lake and caused a sudden storm. The Valley of the Doves — a steep canyon on the west side of the lake — acted like a funnel, trapping the westerly winds and causing them to rush across the shallow waters of Galilee.

The waves poured water into their boat and threatened to sink them. The alarmed apostles frantically bailed out the water and tried to save the boat. Despite all the panic and noise and fear, Jesus slept soundly through it all. The men looked at him, his head resting on a cushion, his face peaceful in the midst of a death dealing storm. How could he possibly sleep? They must wake him and let him know about the danger.

When they gazed at him sleeping they might have remembered the many times their rabbis had told them this is a sign of trust in God. They cited the words of faith to Job, "You shall be secure because there is hope. You shall take your rest with none to disturb" (Job 11:18).

Christian writers were later to compare this scene with a similar one in the book of Jonah. Once again there is a storm. The sailors fight fiercely to save the ship. To their dismay, Jonah sleeps peacefully through it all. Jonah assures them they can be saved if they throw him into the deep. Jonah then goes into the waters of death and into the tomb of the great fish. Three days later he "rises from the dead" on the beach of Niniveh. Greater than Jonah, Jesus is the sleeping, peaceful savior, who will ultimately save the apostles and everyone, by his death and resurrection.

Like the sailors on Jonah's ship, the apostles must enlist the help of the sleeper. In such a crisis all hands must work together. They woke Jesus with a rebuke rising from their own desperation. They seemed to accuse him of indifference to their difficulties. Jesus appeared not to care about them. Has he not abandoned them while they fight the terrors of the sea? He slept. They struggled. These professional fishermen expected everyone to pitch in and save the boat and their lives. Above all, they expected their leader to show concern. Why doesn't he help them when all this force strikes them? "Teacher, do you not care that we are perishing?" (verse 38).

Jesus awoke and rebuked the wind and told the sea to be quiet. Just as he had often warned evil spirits to be quiet, so he commanded the evil spirit of the storm to calm down. Mark writes that this act of Jesus filled them with awe. They had seen him perform many miracles, but they also knew the prophets had done likewise. It seemed incredible to them that he could control a storm. In their minds, God alone had power over the sea and its storms. How often they had prayed the seaman's prayer, "O Lord, you rule over the surging of the sea. You still the swelling of its waves. . . More powerful than the roar of mighty waters, powerful on high is the Lord" (Ps. 89:10; 93:4).

No prophet had ever done anything like this. No magician or wonder-worker was able to still the storm, the most feared enemy of the fisherman. Yet Jesus had done so. He had revealed his identity to them. They needed, however, to move beyond amazement to faith. To be thunderstruck is not enough. The more solid attitude is faith. Feelings of awe diminish. Faith abides. The sound of thunder fades. The silence of faith endures. Jesus looked at their stunned faces and invited them to surpass their oceanic dizziness. Faith is the issue. They must make the transition from wonder to belief. They are not there yet. The journey into faith in Jesus will take more time. Instead they stay at the wonder stage. "Who then is this whom even the wind and sea obey?" (verse 41).

Christians of every age have found great light from this scene of the storm at sea. In the midst of family troubles, arguments, emotional upsets, deaths in the family, wars, economic downturns, persecutions, threats, hostility, Christians felt they were in the storm at sea and that Jesus did not care. He sleeps. They suffer. Then they read this passage again. They have cried out to Christ for help. Jesus once more stills the storm and asks them to have deeper faith.

But Jesus will not take away all the storms of life. Jesus will give every Christian the power and love to make it through the storms. Discipleship will be costly, will require suffering and the Cross. Strong faith in Jesus is the only way to make it through the troubles with inner serenity and courage. Trust in Christ brings the truest security. When that trust exists, nothing can shake us.

Reflection

1. Which holds my attention more, a story or an abstract speech? Why?
2. What benefits could be derived from an oral culture where storytelling was a way of life?
3. Has it ever occurred to me that my education has gradually dulled my capacity for imagination and wonder? Or have I been lucky enough to have an education that nursed it?
4. How could a parable be a divine challenge to me to a conversion of life and deeper faith?
5. Have I ever heard any modern parables? What are some I could share with my friends?
6. Applying the parable of the sower to my life, am I the footpath, the rocky ground, the seed among thorns, or the good ground?
7. Generally speaking, do I find parables easy to grasp?
8. Have I had my own storms at sea? Have I called out to Jesus? What was his response?
9. Can I think of other applications of the storm at sea narrative?

Prayer

Divine storyteller, you capture my imagination and my heart with your parables. You ask me to grow in faith and stay on my faith journey with the love and courage you offer me. Walk with me through all my storms. Then my trust in you will deepen, even when you sleep.

5 Miracles of Compassion

The world is full of God's miracles. Some are extraordinary and supernatural such as those chronicled in the gospels and in the lives of the saints. Some are so ordinary we barely notice them. Scientist Freeman Dyson tells the story of his daughter at camp who found a monarch caterpillar. She put it in a jar and brought it to their New England home. She had found it feeding on the leaves of a milkweed plant. Freeman advised her to put it on the milkweed plant they had in their yard.

After a few days, the caterpillar stopped feeding, hung by its tail and began to squeeze into the skin of its pupa, like a fat boy wriggling into a sleeping bag that is three sizes too small for him. One can barely believe the caterpillar can fit in it. Yet it turns out to be exactly the right size.

Three weeks later a butterfly emerged. Out of the pupa crept the remnant of the caterpillar, much smaller, with wet, black stubs for wings. In the next few minutes, the body dried, the legs stiffened and the wings unfurled. The lovely little creature sprang to life showing off its beauty of orange, black, and white. She took off and flew high over the trees and disappeared into the sky. She had a long trip ahead of her, all the way to the southwest United States — and against the prevailing winds.

She is a miracle, with her tiny brain, a million times smaller than the human brain. With her microscopic clump of nerve tissues she takes charge of her legs and wings, knows how to walk and fly and navigate thousands of miles from the east coast to the Mexican border. A scientist will see her as a miracle of nature's imagination. The psalmist beholds her as one of God's wonders. "The heavens declare the glory of God" (Ps. 19:2).

The Man Who Lived in a Tomb (Mk. 5:1-20)

Just as nature's miracles give us pleasure and move us to praise God, so also do the miracles of Jesus. Not just because of their startling and dramatic quality, but because they reveal the compassion of Jesus for the hurts he found among his people. In the storm at sea, Jesus showed his disciples that he understood they would have to ride out many storms in their faith journey. He felt for them and helped them to see that no storm could overcome them if they trusted him.

The storm has passed and their boat has traveled five miles to the shores of Gerasa in the area of the Ten Cities, or the Decapolis. This is gentile territory. Jesus will now demonstrate that his compassion is meant for gentiles as well as for Jews. Nearby are caves, many of which were used for tombs. Popular belief held that demons haunted those tombs. Thus people connected demons with death. As Jesus stepped off the boat, an inhabitant of those tombs approached him. An unclean spirit possessed this man and dangerously deranged him. Even a chain could not restrain him. He could snap off handcuffs and break the chains used to hold him. No one could tame this maniac. People from the nearby town shuddered at night when they heard his screams from the hillsides and tombs. When they saw him, they could scarcely look at him because he had disfigured himself with sharp rocks. Frightening, he drove them away from him. Pitiful, he could not receive their help because he scared them so much.

Seeing Jesus arrive on the beach, the demon inside the man drove him to Christ's presence. As it neared Jesus, the demon became aware of the intense spiritual force emanating from Christ. The evil spirit forced the man to kneel before Jesus in order to pacify Christ and subvert the unexpected, overwhelming power flowing from Christ's person. As in previous cases, the demon affirmed the divine and messianic identity of Jesus. Moreover, by saying his name, it hoped to gain some control over him. It questioned why Jesus would "meddle" with him.

This will not be an ordinary exorcism, one accomplished with a few words. The man is suffering from a severe form of demonic possession. Jesus will engage in a lengthier process to exorcise this spirit. This will be a process more than a sudden event. The energy and force Jesus exerted on this Gerasa shore symbolized the larger purpose of his ministry, namely, to do battle with the force of evil in the world and conquer it by his death and resurrection.

Compassion moved him to heal this pitiful man. Compassion would also motivate Jesus to heal the deeper human problem, the enchantment with sin and evil. In eradicating the face of evil, Jesus would also erase the root of evil as well. In looking at this depressed man, Jesus saw visibly how evil enslaves people. Such domination by sin may appear less dramatically in most people, but it was there nonetheless.

The difference here is that the man from the tombs could not hide it. The majority of people masked their sins under a veneer of a smiling exterior, a deceptive front. Satan, the father of lies, had done his job well. But Satan's pride tempted him to show off, to stage publicly what he is really all about. Satan intended to master and possess each human person. This poor man was exhibit-A. Jesus, the apostles and the people of Gerasa need only see the demented man, who could not hide the evil that most people are able to conceal. He was a walking advertisement of what sin does to corrode the human person and what it could ultimately accomplish.

The demon inside the man had hoped to control Jesus by knowledge of his name and identity. Jesus turned the table on the demon and asks its name, thus reaching for control over it. The demon replied that it is "Legion." The expression comes from the troops occupying that area, the Roman legion, a detachment of six thousand soldiers, hence dramatizing the depth of the possession.

In this battle between good and evil along the shores of Galilee in gentile territory, Legion slowly realized that the dynamism of Christ is too strong to resist. Knowing that expulsion is imminent and wanting to stay in that locale, the demon asked to be sent into a herd of swine on the nearby cliff. Otherwise, as was popularly thought, Legion would be forced to return to hell. Jesus agreed with the request and gave the word. The multitude of evil spirits entered the swine and drove them berserk, causing them to panic and run into the lake where they drowned.

Some Christians have felt uneasy that the power of Jesus would have a destructive outcome in the killing of the swine. So they interpret this part of the story as a bit of humorous Jewish folklore that Mark has included in the narrative. For them, the tale produces some comic relief in the otherwise somber episode near the graves. No Jew would ever have been herding swine, since that was against the law. And no Jew, therefore, would have shed a tear over a gentile that lost his pigs. The stampede of the swine would thus have been a colorful and entertaining anecdote to be shared around campfires and markets and house gatherings.

Other Christians, noting the wealth of details and the length of the account, conclude that this is an eyewitness story. For them the story of the swine has a deeper meaning beyond any folkloric pleasure it might give. Jesus had not just cured a possessed man. He had purged evil from that land. As the prophet Elijah had once slaughtered the 400 evil prophets of Baal who enslaved God's people, so Jesus now drove out the legion of evil spirits that captivated Galilee of the Gentiles.

In a remarkable way, Jesus brought to life a teaching of Isaiah that the messiah would stretch out his sympathetic heart to a gentile people "living among the graves and spending nights in caverns, eating swine's flesh and crying, 'Hold back! Do not touch me. I am set apart from you!' " (cf. Is. 65:1-5). Jesus thus anticipated the ministry of the apostolic missionaries to that region.

The news spread about the compassionate healing of the crazed man of the tombs. The people came to look for themselves and found the man properly dressed, perfectly sane, and sitting calmly with Jesus. Perversely, the fear they once had of the possessed man falls upon Jesus. They begged him to leave their area. Perhaps his destruction of the herd of swine bothered them more than the trouble from the village maniac.

The healed man then pressed Jesus to accept him as a disciple. Jesus refused. Instead he urged the man to home go to his family and rebuild his life. He could tell them what had happened. But the man wanted to tell the world about Jesus. He traveled all over the Ten Cities proclaiming what Jesus had done for him. He became, in Mark's gospel, the first missionary for Christ to the gentiles. That first evangelizer had once been a madman, crazed by the power of evil. Now he would be a joyful "fool for Christ," liberated by love and ready to share his faith with the Greeks of Decapolis.

Christ's particular triumph over evil at Gerasa forecast his ultimate victory over sin at the cross. The duel on the beach would occur again at the cross, only now with cosmic and universal consequences. The frequency of exorcism stories in this gospel emphasizes this final purpose of Jesus whose goal is to save people from the power and domination of sin. The greatest miracle of all is to be saved from the control of sin and be liberated to practice those values and virtues that make us happy and peaceful and thoroughly human.

An Old Woman and a Girl (Mk. 5:21-43)

Jesus and the apostles returned to the other side of the lake. A synagogue official, named Jairus, came to ask Jesus for a favor. Jairus administered a synagogue. He sounded the ram's horn to summon people to the services, presented the scrolls of the Torah for the readers, and supervised the upkeep of the building. He participated in the selection of men who would lead the sabbath service.

Jairus' twelve-year-old daughter was dying. She might lose her life at the very beginning of her womanhood. Jairus was desperate. His love for his daughter overcame any problem he might have with Jesus. He traveled in the circles of religious leaders who had circulated the message that the Galilean preacher was a dangerous person. He was upsetting the religious order of things, broke sabbath laws, and even claimed to forgive sins.

But Jairus had also heard that Jesus could cure people. No one was more precious to him than his daughter. If he had to break ranks with his peers, so be it. In this life and death crisis, Jairus put aside any misgivings he might have about Jesus and went to him to ask for a cure. He threw himself on the ground before Christ and made his earnest appeal. He humbled himself like a slave before a master and begged for a favor. Love moved him to cast aside all thought of appearances. What difference is dignity going to make if his daughter were to lose her life?

He swallowed his pride and prayed for a healing. He asked Jesus to come and lay hands upon his daughter that she might "get well and live." Healers and physicians have always known the value of touch in the hands. The hands can caress and stroke to calm a person down. The hands can feel certain signs and causes of an illness. The hands sometimes can heal.

In our own times the magic of touch has come to the foreground. Bumper stickers say, "Have you hugged your child today?" Those who work with alienated juveniles note that these young people have starved for affectionate touch from their parents and did not receive it. People with the gift of healing from the Holy Spirit spontaneously resort to the laying on of hands. Biblical people, such as Jairus, knew very well the warm balm of touch and freely asked for it.

Jairus also asked that his daughter might get well and live. He asked for a physical cure. Christians ever since have also seen in these words a deeper meaning, that one may rise from the dead to eternal life. Jairus' daughter may rise from sickness and live to be a woman with the usual life span. A Christian hopes that, with Christ's grace, he or she will rise from death and enjoy eternal life. It so happens that Mark's words in the Greek possess both meanings.

Jairus has touched Jesus' heart and the two of them leave for the home of the synagogue official. The crowd came along, pushing closely against Jesus. There was a woman in the crowd who had suffered from vaginal bleeding for twelve years. This not only caused physical discomfort but also rendered her ritually unclean. "When a woman is afflicted with a flow of blood for several days outside her menstrual period . . . as long as she suffers this unclean flow, she shall be unclean, just as during her menstrual period" (Lv. 15:25).

Hence she suffered a spiritual problem as well. She had all the problems of pain along with the religious isolation caused by this illness. And now she was also broke. She had tried many doctors and used up all her savings in the process. But no doctor helped her. At the end of her rope, she decided to reach out and touch the robe of Jesus. What did she have to lose? Jesus would not notice her touching his cloak with so many people jostling against him. She did this anonymously, because as an unclean woman she would be "defiling" Christ in the process.

Her plan worked. She felt the flow dry up immediately. Jesus noticed that healing power had flowed from him. He stopped and asked who touched him. The puzzled apostles said that dozens of people had been pushing against him all along. Why should he ask such a question? But Jesus wanted people to understand that it was the faith of the woman that opened her to a cure, not an automatic, magic-like touching of his clothing.

She was bound to tell her relatives and friends what had happened. Jesus made sure that everyone realized the true source of the miracle. He was not a totem that one felt for the purpose of deriving mysterious power. He would not approve of nor foster popular superstition. Miracles were interpersonal events, not the result of charms and good-luck clothing. Jesus was a person who responded with merciful love to those who touched him with faith.

The poor woman was terrified. She feared that she had offended Jesus and that the miracle would be withdrawn. Shaking with apprehension she came forward, knelt before him, and told him the truth. Jesus smiled at her, lifted her up and gave her a hug. He told her, loud enough for all to hear, that it was her faith that had cured her. Affectionately calling her "daughter," he bade her go in peace and said that she would be free of her illness. To round matters off, his words to her also meant that her faith brought her salvation from her sins. She had clearly tapped the wells of the kindness and sensitivity of Christ.

At that moment messengers from Jairus' house came with the tragic report that his daughter had died. There will be no need to bother Jesus any further. Privately, they may have been relieved, for they might not have approved of involving Jesus in this matter. Possibly, they doubted Jesus could have raised her from the dead. Probably, they did not want their master to be associated with this man of whom other religious leaders disapproved. Jesus responds with a magnificent guideline for all Christians. "Fear is useless. What is needed is trust" (verse 36).

By speaking of fear, Jesus identified the attitude that undermines genuine religion. Jesus is not talking about the fear that is really awe and reverence. That is the source of wisdom. He refers to the fear that is an anxiety to please, an attitude of timidity that cancels all risk, a feeling of fright that paralyzes action. Why is fear useless? Because it forbids the very love that is the essence of God and the result of salvation. Jesus offers the love that cancels such fear. He says it is better to trust than to fear. If Jesus himself were to live by fear he would never make it through the Garden of Gethsemane. If fear ruled him, he would walk away from the cross. He will feel fear, but he will never let it guide him.

Arrived at the house, the group heard the wailing and the other sounds of mourning. The professional mourners had arrived to join the family's own weeping. Jesus ordered them all to keep quiet. The girl's death is only a sleep from which one will be awakened at the resurrection. In the hysteria of the moment, they turn from wails to jeers. They laughed at him and ridiculed his teaching. Jesus became stern, set boundaries, and told them all to leave the house.

He would only allow the parents and his apostles to enter the sick room. Jesus paused and looked at the face of death in the features of that young girl. This was one of his three enemies, the others being illness and sin. He, who had wrestled with Legion at Gerasa, now looked into the eyes of death and overcame its hold. He took the girl's hand and asked her to get up. She rose from the dead. Immediately, she began walking around, embracing her parents and kissing them. Jesus, knowing how hungry twelve-year-olds can be, said, "Give her something to eat." And that home rang with God's praises.

Reflection

1. Christ's supernatural miracles are carefully detailed in the gospels. What are some ordinary miracles of everyday life?
2. What are the purposes of Christ's miracles?
3. How does the exorcism of the man from the tombs at Gerasa differ from earlier exorcisms of Christ?
4. What are some details in the exorcism story that remind one of a horror story?
5. How is this exorcism more clearly a dress rehearsal for the saving act of Christ at Calvary?
6. Has there been a time in my life when I, like Jairus, have come to Christ out of desperation, abandoning conventional dignity, to pour out my heart to the Lord?

7. What is there about a life and death crisis that alters our normal behavior?
8. Jesus had cured the woman with the flow of blood. Why did he insist that the miracle be made public?
9. Do I empathize with Christ's dismay over the lack of sense among the mourners at the little girl's house?
10. What are the three enemies Jesus came to conquer?

Prayer

Compassionate Jesus, you enfolded the man from the tombs, the woman with the flow of blood, and the little girl with your saving healing and your saving grace. You offer all of us your mercy, not just for our mental, emotional, and physical well being, but also for our soul's health. I pray for the kind of faith witnessed by all these good people. I believe. Help my unbelief.

6   Christ Upon the Waters

Family Problems (Mk. 6:1-6)

We saw how Christ's family tried to restrain him because they worried about his mental stability and disliked the negative impact his ministry had on their reputation. They wanted him home in Nazareth where they could control him. Jesus had other ideas and rebuffed their attempt to rein him in. He continued his ministry of parables and miracles. He even left Jewish territory for a brief mission to the gentiles in Gerasa, where he won a duel with an evil Legion on the beach of that gentile settlement.

Now at last he was ready to go home for a visit. But this will be more than a family reunion. Like a well trained athlete toned to the height of his powers, Jesus always put his mission first. That was a non-negotiable commitment. His family would have to accept that. It would cause them to sit in the synagogue and steam when the hometown folks repudiated him.

The people rejected him because their local snobbery could not accept the fact the mere son of a carpenter could deliver such wisdom and mighty works. Perversely, they assumed that no one in his class should speak and act with the authority he displayed. They wanted no manual laborer being so pretentious.

Jesus never became defensive about his working-man background. Most of his adult life he had labored as a carpenter. He knew how to identify with and respect the working man. He neither promoted class conflict, nor did he let a caste system hem him in, for he moved freely among the mighty and the lowly alike. He loved work in all its variety because he envisioned it as a share in the divine work of creation. Honest work continued God's creative initiative.

The people of Nazareth put him down, partly out of local snobbery and mostly because he called them to religious and moral conversion. He preached the Gospel of salvation to them. He afflicted their consciences about their sinfulness and the need for spiritual change, openness to divine forgiveness, and the call to witness the kingdom of love and justice in the world. He spoke to them like a prophet would. But prophets do not succeed among their own people. They walked away from more than what they presumed was an upstart. They turned their backs on a savior.

The reference in the text to the brothers and sisters of Jesus is really to his cousins. Jesus is the only son of Mary. The church teaches that Mary had only one child, and that was a son, and that Mary was always a virgin.

The Mission (Mk. 6:7-13)

The negative Nazareth response did not slow the pace of Jesus' mission. He assembled his apostles and trained them to do some missionary work themselves. He admonished them to "shake the dust from their feet" and leave a group that refuses the love and forgiveness offered in his Gospel. God created us without asking our permission. But God will not save us unless we permit divine love to do so. That is exactly what had happened at Nazareth. It is better to move on and share our faith with those who hunger for God and will accept Christ.

His words about traveling light reminded these missionary trainees to have a spirit of freedom from possessions, which releases them to depend on God. This is symbolized by their depending on others for charity. Jesus would say that a laborer deserves compensation for his work. Mission effort is a form of work. While it is true that St. Paul earned a living from his tent-making, he did so to stop those critics who might accuse him of preaching the gospel just to make money.

The money scandals associated with some TV preachers, as well as mismanagement of funds by some church agencies, are cautionary tales that prove how wise and correct Christ's teaching on money and mission was and still is.

Jesus taught his apostles to anoint the sick with oil. In time this practice would be an essential ritual of the Sacrament of Anointing. The oil signifies the healing of the person preparing for eternal life as well as physical healing in some cases.

Herod Executes the Baptist (Mk. 6:14-29)

News came to Jesus about the martyrdom of his cousin, John the Baptist. Herod had jailed John for publicly condemning his adulterous marriage to his brother's wife. He also feared John would organize his followers into an armed revolt against him. At the same time, the Baptist fascinated him. He was reluctant to do more than imprison him at the royal fortress of Machaerus near the Dead Sea.

His wife, Herodias, wanted John dead. Her chance came at the king's birthday banquet. Her daughter danced so magnificently that the dazed and enchanted monarch promised her any gift she would like. Herodias prompted her to ask for the head of the Baptist on a platter. Herod hated the idea but felt obliged to keep his promise. So the gruesome act was played out like a horror scene from a Stephen King novel. The ceremony of passing a plate with a human head on it from the soldier, to the dancer to the mother underscored the corruption of the court. John's martyrdom anticipated the deadly fate Jesus would face and the high cost of discipleship the apostles would endure. John had prepared the people for a messiah. He also heralded Christ's death. Jesus is never far from the cross.

Bread in the Wilderness (Mk. 6:33-44)

The apostles returned from their mission duty. They told Jesus that people kept them so busy there was hardly time to eat. Jesus said they all needed a retreat, a time for peace and quiet and prayerful renewal. Christian ministry is a mixture of activity and creative inactivity. There is a time to speak and a time to listen. Too much ministry becomes an obsession. No ministering at all would be a lack of responsibility.

Natural activists (parish work horses) revel so much in church work that they burn out. They have nothing inside to give, so they give up. Natural passives spend so much time on over-preparing for ministry like professional students that fears about failure stop them from sharing Christ's love. The body of the apostolate is ministry. The soul of ministry is the renewing juices of prayer, silence, and contemplation.

The apostolic party sailed to a retreat area in the desert only to find the crowds there to meet them. Their retreat was put on hold. Jesus felt great sympathy for these people for they were like sheep without a shepherd. They craved spiritual food and were hungry. They yearned for spiritual leadership, but the leaders were more interested in their own agendas than people's real needs.

Every period of church history voices the same complaint. Leaderless Christians will hunger for God and not be fed. They will cry out for leadership but be left to fend for themselves. The young suffer the most from this neglect. They have so little experience from which to draw and not enough background to judge what is healthy for them. This fact challenges the modern church as much as it did any other age of the church.

Late that afternoon, the apostles urged Jesus to send the people home to eat. Jesus told them to feed the people. How was this possible with so little money and only a few loaves and fishes? Jesus told them to bring him the food. Jesus took the bread, looked up to heaven and blessed the bread, broke it and gave it to the people.

As God once fed Israel with manna in the desert, Jesus now fed 5,000 people in a wilderness. His act looked back in time to the divine love that fed the hungry. His deed looked forward in time to life in God's kingdom where the messiah will preside at a banquet of love. His gestures of taking, blessing, breaking, and giving of the bread remind us of what he will do at the Last Supper. He already evokes the images of that great supper and the messianic banquet, both of which will be celebrated in the Eucharists of the early church, as well as our own today. The bread miracle is the most loved and most popular of all Christ's miracles, being reported in all four gospels and twice in Mark.

The four acts of Jesus in the bread miracle — taking, blessing, breaking, and giving — illustrate four steps in becoming Christ's disciple. (1) Take. Jesus did wonders with so little. Divine love made a banquet out of a few rolls. His love took the raw material of a few apostles and initiated a world mission. Divine love can take each of us, with even the smallest talent, and create a power for love, justice, and peace in the world. We can take the bread of love which God has planted in our hearts and do so much with it. Someone has said that love is like the five loaves and two fishes. It does not start to multiply until it is given away.

(2) Bless. Jesus blesses our lives. This makes us ready for mission. This brings our lives within the radiant love of God that transforms them from lives without meaning and purpose to ones with a goal and a destiny. The wick of a candle is dry and static until the flame makes it shine and give light. The blessing of love introduces the dynamic into our lives. It enables us to discover that we are limitless drives to love and be loved. We are meant to be more than driftwood floating aimlessly down the river of life. Christ's blessing sets our wooden intentions on fire and makes them burn with purpose.

Then we are a blessing to others. We set them on fire with our enthusiasms, a word that comes from the Greek *en-theos* meaning the God within. Our faith sharing becomes a blessing to those who are lucky to experience it. We offer the spark that makes community possible and friendship a reality. We bless others when we hold them in our hearts.

(3) Break. Jesus broke the bread of his body that the love of his person might be revealed. Anyone who has ever had a great love for another knows that sorrow and tears and suffering go with the territory. No great and true love has ever existed without pain as the cost. When Jesus broke the bread in the desert and again at the Last Supper, he did more than separate some crusts of a loaf, he was thinking of love and its most radical demands. It has been said that the only way one knows he or she has a heart, is that it has to be broken first. The strongest and truest love is purchased at the price of sacrifice.

We, too, must allow the breaking of the bread of our bodies — meaning our whole selves — to let love flow from us to others. Often that is done by the very people we try to love. They may break our hearts, but how else can we show them we love them? This is not a call for self pity, nor a sentimental regret over a love lost. It is the affirmation that we must let our pain open us to let out the deepest love that lies within us. It is an act of faith in love's ability to transform others, not for our gratification, but for the happiness that we so profoundly wish for others. It is never a weakness, but always an act of rock-like strength.

(4) Give. Jesus gave away so much bread that twelve baskets were collected afterward. Love multiplied in the giving. Hoarding love for special occasions dries it up. No one ever understood the value of giving more than Jesus. We associate the word gift with Christ more readily than any other person. That is why the term grace so readily comes to mind when contemplating Christ. He is Gift-Grace.

Because we have now gone through the process of love, the taking-blessing-breaking, we reach the point of the whole action-giving. It is time to share. In a world that is always "on the take" we counter the culture by being "on the give." At the heart of it all is our lives as gifts. Hence, this is not a matter of giving things and money, though that may happen. Unless we give our persons in the form of love, anything else we offer does not shine with love. That is why Jesus would finally say bluntly at the Last Supper, when he passed around the bread, "This is I. This is my person. This is my Body — Me."

Christ Upon the Waters (Mk. 6:45-56)

Jesus then sent the apostles to Bethsaida by boat, while he retired to the mountain to pray. This communion with God, following the bread miracle and preceding the walking on the waters, reveals that God is the source of what he is doing. Just before dawn, at the fourth watch of the night, Jesus looked out over the lake from his mountain post. He saw his apostles, still at sea, struggling against a strong and treacherous wind. They needed him.

Prayer did not close him from human need. It opened him to human thirsts and hungers. Jesus walked through that storm and across the waters to save them. The frightened apostles think they see a ghost, much as they will again when they behold his resurrected presence. Jesus removed their fear and astonished them once more by subduing the winds.

The gospel writers love to link the story of Christ upon the waters with the bread miracle. In Scripture, the prophets viewed the feeding of hungry multitudes as a messianic act. On the other hand, walking on the waters could only be an act of God who alone could control the winds and the waves. Like God, Jesus crossed the waters and said to them, "It is I." That expression is similar to the one God spoke to Moses from the burning bush, "I Am." Jesus performed both a messianic and a divine deed.

Jesus offered these revelations to his apostles as part of their training. They witnessed his most striking sharing of himself with them. He did not tell them who he was. He showed them. He provided them with awesome experiences of his love and inner nature. Each event was an invitation to faith. Then he left them in their freedom. He would not force their faith. Jesus trusted in the process that moved them along their faith journey in the halting steps that were true to their human natures.

For most people, conversion to Jesus is rarely a blinding Damascus experience. It is a slow, often frustrating, story of three steps forward and two steps backward. Like a farmer, Jesus has planted the seed of faith in the earth of their hearts and permitted the mystery of growth to unfold.

The apostles experienced these revelations with fear and wonder. Twice now they have beheld him as Christ-upon-the-waters, in the sense of mastering the winds and waves. Twice, in Mark's gospel, they will watch him perform a bread miracle. Yet in none of these cases will their faith arise to confess him as Messiah and Son of God. Mark comments bluntly on how they failed to come to faith, "their hearts were hardened" (verse 52).

They do not reflect as yet on these revelations with faith. Ideally, they should have sung divine praises. Instead they settle for amazement, astonishment, wonder — proper responses indeed, but far short of the faith that sings the mighty power of God. Their faith journey is at its infant stage. They like and trust Jesus as a person, a leader who helps them appreciate themselves, a healer who does a lot of good, a teacher who broadens their horizons. But they do not yet realize who he really is.

The growing opposition Jesus will soon face will shake their confidence in him. The crucifixion will virtually shatter what little faith they have acquired. Only in the light of the resurrection and the coming of the Holy Spirit will their faith look back on his teachings and mighty works and realize how all this described his true identity as Messiah and Son of God. Then, paradoxically, they will behold the cross as a supreme revelation of his love and identity.

Reflection

1. Is there a prophet in my family, circle of friends, or in my parish who is not accepted? How should I respond?
2. Why is it important for church ministers to be detached from money and material preoccupations?
3. Is the Sacrament of Anointing only meant for those who are dying?
4. The apostles are exhausted by their first missionary activity. What is Jesus' cure for this?
5. What happens to those who burn out in ministry? What generally causes the burnout?
6. Can I identify cases today in my local church where I see "sheep without a shepherd?" Am I part of the problem?
7. What aspects of the bread miracle narrative remind me of the Eucharist?
8. Would prayer make me avoid people's problems or open me to empathize with them?
9. What does the narrative of Christ-upon-the-waters say to me?
10. Why did the apostles miss the revelations of the bread miracle and Christ-upon-the-waters? In other words, why did they not come to faith in these revelations at the time they happened?

Prayer

Jesus, my shepherd, you always look out for me. You feed me with love and give me your Spirit to guide and teach me. Turn me toward you that my faith may see more clearly and move me to accept what you offer me.

7 Love in the Food

Do I Want a Static or Dynamic Sense of Self? (Mk. 7:1-23)

An Italian lady in a large mideastern city runs a popular restaurant in the traditional Italian style. She has placed a statue of St.
Joseph in the middle of the dining area and every St. Joseph's day
(March 19) she serves free meals for the poor. Impressed by her earthy wisdom, one of her priest friends likes to get her point of view on
pastoral problems he faces. One day he asked her, "Momma, why do
people get divorced?" "TV," was her prompt reply. "Be serious,"
countered the priest. "All right, I'll tell you," she responded. "The
problem with couples today is there's no love in the sex, no love in
the talk — and no love in the food."

Her folksy saying, so full of truth, applies very well to the kind
of religion Jesus faced in his confrontation with the delegation of
Pharisees who came from Jerusalem to meet with him. In effect,
Jesus tried to tell them, "There's no love in your religious point of
view."

The Pharisees challenged him to explain why his disciples did
not perform the ritual washings before eating. They were not talking
about hygiene, but religious purification rites. Washing hands from
the day's accumulated grime was different from washing them ritually, the latter being a symbolic form of spiritual cleansing. This was
the theory. Jesus showed how the practice had degenerated.

Every Jewish home possessed a stone jar of ritually clean water
— something like holy water — which was used only for these
ceremonies. A person held his or her hands with the tips of the
fingers pointed upward, while water was poured over them. Then the
person took the fist of one hand and rubbed it against the other for
the "washing." But now the water was unclean because it had
touched unclean hands, so the tips of the hands were turned

downwards and water poured on them again to complete the ceremony. The same process was used for cups, pots, and pans. They were first washed for the usual purpose and then they were washed ritually. The practice had become a tedious burden and had lost its meaning.

Jesus shocked them by neglecting these customary rites and instructing his followers to do the same. They asked him why his disciples did not live according to the tradition of the elders. Jesus called them hypocrites, a term that applied to an actor whose face was hidden behind a mask. He accused them of ignoring the commandments of God and forcing everyone to obey human commandments. They had elevated customs invented by humans to the dignity of a divine commandment with the result that human law replaced divine precepts.

He reminded them that he was not the first one to level such a judgement. Centuries ago, Isaiah had said the same thing (Is. 29:13). When the human heart strays from a loving relationship with God, then the divine law will be set aside and human rules will be substituted for it. The ten commandments were meant to be liberating values that enhanced human development and showed the heart how to love God, self, and others.

The numerous, tiresome rules of human origin, which they imposed, oppressed people. God's law released energy to love. These human customs, wrongly cloaked with so-called divine approval, closed off the creative power of love and replaced it with the love of power. In so acting, they taught people to have a static view of self. This engraved in every mind the question, "What am I supposed to do?"

This meant that a person's moral identity was in terms of function. "I am what I do." Pushed by this vision of life, the person lives by externals alone. Life becomes a cold ledger wherein good and bad deeds are tallied up in the hope that the credits outweigh the debits. This is the religion of the bottom line. Gradually, hearts drift far from God. All sense of interiority is lost. What should have been spirituality became "materiality."

There can be no spiritual growth or self fulfillment in God, because there is no internal drama going on. The pious rituals originally were meant to support obedience to the commandments and a surrender to divine love. By replacing the commandments, these customs — traditions of the elders — stalled the human spirit in the dead end of the static self.

Jesus rediscovered for his listeners the role of the dynamic view of self. "Who am I? Who should I become?" If I sin, I am doing more than breaking a rule. I am ruining a relationship. I am breaking love. I am harming persons. I am arresting my own personal growth. In the dynamic view of self, the attention turns inward to the movements of the heart. Awareness of one's relationship to God, one rooted in love, comes to the foreground. Rules, customs, and laws become background, not forgotten, but properly subordinated to the love affair of the heart that is underway.

The static self enslaves the person to the drudgery of obeying a law for its own sake. The dynamic self makes a human free to obey tne person of God in love. A rule, law, or custom simply becomes a way to do this. A religion based on the static self causes one to be a hypocrite, one who play-acts at faith but never really believes since no divine-human encounter is going on. The heart is far from God. A religion based on the dynamic vision of self enables one to be a true believer, embarked on the journey of faith and committed to the adventure of love.

Jesus illustrated his criticism of them by showing how they allowed the purpose of God's fourth commandment to be replaced by one of their human customs. It was understood that if someone made a donation of money or property to the temple for its upkeep and administration, that was considered a gift made to God. The official certification of the gift was called "Corban." Originally, this was an innocent enough and straight forward transaction. The donation was made and certified as Corban and it could not be dedicated to any other use. By Christ's time, however, the custom was used as a cover-up to protect one from fulfilling one's financial obligations either to one's parents or to a creditor.

In collusion with temple administrators, a fee was paid to the treasury in return for the Corban seal that exempted certain monies and properties from being seized by a creditor or claimed by elderly parents for their survival. Ostensibly, the money or property had all been given to the temple. In fact only a user fee, a kind of religious bribery, was transmitted.

It was clear to everyone that the original meaning of the fourth commandment concerned the care and support of one's parents in their old age. (Yes, it also involved the proper attitudes of little children toward their parents.) Surrounding nomadic societies had practiced the abandonment of elderly parents when they could no longer easily travel with the tribe. But Israel should not resemble such heartless people. God's people should assume responsibility for the elderly.

Hence the adult children of elderly parents were expected to support them. The misuse of the Corban rule created irresponsible adult children. Corban was invented as an act of piety. Here it is perverted into an act of filial impiety. Worse yet, this act of impiety was used to replace God's fourth commandment. A custom based on *un*love substituted for God's law based on love and respect for one's parents. The "tradition of the elders" made void the voice of God (verse 13).

Jesus wanted the Pharisees to rediscover the religion of the heart, which was deep in the truest tradition of their people, going all the way back to the covenant at Sinai. He saw he was not making much headway with them, so he turned back to the people and gave them a teaching on the religion of the heart. Using the example of ritual cleansing and its externalism, he asked them to look at the issue from the opposite view.

Presumably, whatever was purified and entered their bodies, would not defile them. But suppose they ate unclean foods. Did such food really harm them spiritually? The people could have argued with him that their ancestors had gone to martyrdom rather than eat unclean food (cf. Maccabees). Nonetheless, Jesus forged ahead and startled them by saying that what goes into a person's body does not defile. It simply enters the stomach, is digested and passes on. *It does not touch the heart.*

It is what comes out of a person's heart that really causes trouble. Jesus then listed thirteen vices that flow from a sinful heart. His point was that people should be far more concerned about the vicious behavior flowing from a corrupted heart than the fussy, nitpicking preoccupation with ritually clean foods and cleansing ceremonies. Is a soiled hand more sinful than a liar's lips? Is a taboo porkchop more evil than a murderer's eyes? Is a spotted cup more repulsive than a heart filled with lust?

The incongruity was self evident. The Pharisees were not amused by what may have seemed a clever comment on their superficiality. They knew what he was saying and disagreed with it. They really did believe that their human laws, in some crazy way, either had superseded the commandments or at the very least had become God's will for them.

As to the apostles and the common folk, the words of Jesus were obviously upsetting. His teachings were so radically new and different from what their religious culture required of them every hour of every day, they could not begin to imagine living by them. They probably agreed with him that an evil heart causes all their troubles. But they were clearly not so ready to abandon the rituals of purification and begin to eat unclean foods.

They kept on following these rules until the gentile Christian converts challenged them by citing Christ's teaching on the matter. In fact it would take a vision granted to Peter after Pentecost to shake him loose from his lifelong attachment to these rules and customs (cf. Acts 10:10-16). Even then it took a major summit meeting of Christian leaders at Jerusalem to solve the matter (cf. Acts 15). It took time, experience, and the guidance of the Holy Spirit for the Christian community to grasp the meaning and application of the Lord's instructions.

The Woman Was a Greek (Mk. 7:24-37)

Pursuing as ever the rhythm of involvement and withdrawal, of intense ministry followed by retreat and reflection, Jesus led the apostles to the region of Tyre and Sidon in Phoenicia — presently, southern Lebanon. The last time he had entered gentile territory was at Gerasa, the Galilee of the gentiles.

Just when he thought he would enjoy a temporary break from his ministry, Jesus was approached by a Greek woman, a Syrophoenician by birth. She begged him to cast out the demon from her daughter. Jesus told her the children of Israel must be fed first. The bread of children should not be given to dogs.

His two remarks are puzzling. Had he not already ministered in gentile Gerasa and exorcised a demon so great it was called Legion? Moreover, he seemed quite willing to stay there for a time of further ministry and only left because the local people wanted him to. He obviously was willing to minister to gentiles there. Why not here? Why is he suddenly reluctant to serve this woman for a healing evidently simpler than the one for the man from the tombs? Secondly, why did he use the troubling image of a dog to make his point?

Small clues offer some light. He told the woman that the Jews were his first mission priority. This implied that others would later become the beneficiaries of Christian mission activity. As God's first covenant people, Israel deserved the first announcement of the Gospel.

Then there is the unsettling symbolism of the dog. Greeks used the term for a brassy, shameless woman, not unlike the similar epithets in our own culture. Jews also used the word dog to express contempt. These cultures based that image on the stray, scrawny, often vicious dogs of the street — wild dogs that caused trouble, bit people and gave them rabies.

On the other hand, there is the house dog, the pet puppy, the beloved dog that is a human's best friend. Jesus used this softer, milder "house pet" reference when he spoke to the woman. From this one can infer that Jesus spoke to her with a friendly tone of voice and a look on his face that did not put her off.

The outcome of the story seems to support this view. Despite her desperate, maternal agony, she playfully took his use of the word puppies and reminded him that they eagerly and happily waited for food from the table. Better yet, the family usually complied. Jesus loved her for her skillful and witty reply. At that moment he drove the demon from her daughter and told the mother to go home and find a healthy girl — which she did.

Gentile Christian converts of the New Testament church would love hearing this story preached at their gatherings. They could identify with the feisty woman and feel very much at home in the community of the redeemed.

Jesus and his apostles then traveled extensively in gentile territory, finally arriving at Decapolis. A deaf man, who also had a speech impediment, was brought to him for healing. While Jesus was always personal in performing his miracles, seldom was he so explicit about it as in this healing. He knew the man could not hear him and would normally communicate through signs.

Jesus took him aside from the distractions of the crowd and used signs that the man would appreciate. He touched the man's ears. He took some of his spittle and touched the man's tongue. Popular belief held there was a healing quality to spittle. The deaf man then saw Jesus look up to the sky and let out a deep sigh.

In other words, Jesus provided body talk for a man who might otherwise not know what Jesus was communicating. Finally, he saw Jesus' lips move. Jesus said, "Ephphata," which means, "Be opened." Suddenly, the man could hear and speak. Once again Jesus demonstrated that a miracle was an act of communion, an interpersonal event. Here, as in virtually all the miracle stories, the spectators are amazed and filled with wonder. The one healed has always responded in faith. Those who see the wonders, however, simply wonder. They have not yet reached the stage of faith commitment and discipleship.

Reflection

1. Am I the type of person who settles for the practices of religion without ever moving through and beyond them to a deeper relationship with Jesus?
2. Have I been able to tell the difference between accumulated religious practices, resulting from history and customs, and the essential attitudes and practices willed by God?
3. Why were the apostles so slow to accept Jesus' teachings about food laws and ritual cleansings?
4. Behavior modification techniques do help some people overcome certain problems such as addictive smoking. But Jesus teaches that "heart modification" is needed to overcome the thirteen vices he lists in his teachings (verse 21-22). How do I react to this?

5. How can I bring about "heart modification" regarding any of the thirteen vices that may exist in my life?
6. Was Jesus too hard on the Pharisees? Were they being too hard on him? Would extended negotiations have helped resolve their conflicts?
7. Have I had difficulty interpreting the approach Jesus took to the Greek woman, a Syrophoenician by birth?
8. Why did Jesus insist that the Gospel first be preached to Jews?
9. Do I see why Jesus used body talk in his healing of the deaf man who had a speech impediment?
10. Christ's miracles caused awe and wonder in the spectators. Why did they not also cause faith and discipleship? Is the act of wonder a preliminary preparation for faith? Psychologically, does the process of wonder feel a lot like faith? Is it an act of personal commitment, or is it too distant?

Prayer

Greater than all prophets, dear Lord, you repeated the teachings of the prophets about the religion of the heart. Your saving death would provide the transforming power that changed hearts and make your teachings truly effective. I ask again and again for this gift of heart conversion so that my life will witness positive virtues and not destructive vices. I praise you for this grace.

8 Social Ministry Complements Spiritual Ministry

Bread Miracle for Gentiles (Mk. 8:1-21)

Isak Dinesen's short story, "Babette's Feast," echoes the touching generosity found in the bread miracle stories of the gospels. Set in a tiny, remote Danish fishing village, the story tells of Martina and Phillipa, daughters of the founder of a devout religious sect. Both women had sacrificed love and marriage to carry on the work of their deceased father.

Only twelve members of the sect remain. The aging group tends to be quarrelsome and apathetic. One stormy night, a French refugee woman, Babette, arrives at the sisters' door. She asks for room and board. In return she would cook for them and clean the house. Somewhat reluctant and suspicious, the sisters agree to try this out. As time passes, Babette proves to be a perfect addition to their household.

Some time later, Babette receives news that she has won the Paris lottery — a sum of ten thousand francs. Coincidentally, the sect was looking for a way to celebrate the hundredth anniversary of their beloved founder. Babette suggests that she use her winnings to prepare them a feast worthy of the occasion. The grateful community accepts her offer.

Then troubling things occur. Cases of wine arrive from Paris. Crates of shiny, dark skinned turtles come from a seaport. Strange and exotic foods fill Babette's kitchen. The spartan, abstemious religious group had never touched alcohol and observed a simple diet in keeping with their austere ideals. Fearful, they peek into Babette's domain and believe they see a witches' brew steaming.

They hold a private council to determine what they should do. Matters had advanced too far to stop the feast. They decided to go ahead with it, but resolved they would not speak a word to Babette about her cooking. No compliments. No condemnations.

The great night arrived. The twelve sat down to feast. It turned out there was an extra guest, the son of one of the members — and a former suitor for Martina. He was a military officer, world traveled and sophisticated. As each course of Babette's feast appeared at their table, the officer loudly praised this magnificent gourmet meal. Only one other time had he dined as well, and that was at a Parisian restaurant where such a meal cost ten thousand francs. (It was Babette's restaurant where she presided before a revolution caused her to flee.)

After many glasses of superb wine and numerous plates of flavorful food, amid the golden candlelight, the stern little group mellowed, began to smile, laugh, and forgive each other for the petty insults of recent times. They remembered their founder with affection. At the end of the meal, they joined hands, resolved to be friends again, and danced in the village street by the light of the moon.

Martina and Phillipa went to the kitchen to thank Babette. They said they hoped she would find happiness in her future with her new found money. The unworldly sisters had no idea how much their meal had cost. Babette told them she had spent all her money on the feast. She had given them everything she had, her money, her cooking artistry, her affection for them. The story ends with the fumbling and grateful silence of the sisters. After all, what words could match the love Babette had brought them?

Such also is the message of the bread miracles of Jesus. They are his signs of affection for a world that hungers for love. He made that clear when he said, "My heart is moved with pity for the crowd" (verse 2). His interest in ministering to their physical hunger would be matched by his concern for their soul hungers. Jesus always addressed the needs of the total person. He was not above thinking about people's ordinary physical needs.

Some Christians think their only calling is to alleviate the social problems of our time. They have a gift for doing this. But occasionally their excitement blinds them from realizing that people have spiritual hungers as well. The oppressed need to be saved from their own sins as well as those of society. The deprived yearn for union with God as well as integration into the social order.

Other Christians have a talent for speaking to the spiritual thirsts of people, but show little interest in their social problems and experiences of injustice. Social ministry and spiritual ministry must go together. The social side of the Gospel and its spiritual aspect should complement each other.

The Civil Rights Movement in the United States won a stunning achievement politically and legally. New structures of justice were enacted. But many now experience the bitter aftertaste of continued racism. Why? Because there is yet another phase — the spiritual conversion of hearts still filled with prejudice. It was certainly hard to change bad laws into good ones. It is even more challenging to change biased hearts into hearts of compassion, love, and understanding.

Moses liberated his people from the injustices of Egypt and led them to freedom in the desert. That was a fantastic act of social ministry. Then he realized his people had spiritual problems. The problems of freedom tempted them to yearn for the flesh pots of Egypt. Spiritually immature, they hated the risks and uncertainties of a dangerous and threatening desert. They began to prefer slavery to freedom. Yes, they were freed from political oppression. They needed to be liberated for a satisfying covenant with God. Moses had to convince them they should be open to spiritual conversion and change.

Jesus never believed that filling people's stomachs was enough. He knew their spiritual requirements were equally important. At the same time, Christ's compassion was practical, not theoretical. He did not agonize with the words, "Would that something could be done." He sensibly set about doing what had to be done, namely, feeding hungry people.

The first bread miracle was performed for Jews. The second one was for gentiles, 4,000 of them in the region of Decapolis. They possibly heard the enthusiastic story of the cured demoniac from his own lips. Impressed by his enthusiasm, they came to hear Jesus for themselves. It is not difficult to imagine that he was one of the happy participants in Christ's feast at Decapolis.

Back in Galilee, Jesus had another argument with the Pharisees. They had heard of the second bread miracle and decided to bait and badger him by asking him for a "real" sign from heaven. They knew perfectly well he had performed countless miracles. Since they did not believe he was truly a prophet, they dismissed his miracles as the product of a better than average wonder-worker. The extremists among them accused him of using diabolical power for these wonders.

All of his miracles were signs from heaven. Each miracle offered people the opportunity to have faith in Christ. Miracles did not prove who Christ was unless one had faith. Praise God first and then the deeds will prove the presence of God's power. Cynicism cloaked the Pharisees' request for a sign from heaven. They had witnessed Christ's powers and concluded his signs came from an evil source.

Now they dared Christ to try and convince them with some kind of sign that would prove he represented God. Jesus looked at them, shook his head with sadness and frustration, sighed deeply in his spirit, and told them that their generation will never get a sign. God knows he had tried. No miracle would convince them. Their minds were made up. As the old saying puts it, "A man against his will is of the same opinion still."

Slow Apostles

Every parent and every teacher knows how hard it is to get a point across. Evidence abounds. Instructions and explanations are repeated endlessly. Still the child seems dense. Again the student fails to comprehend. It may console parents and teachers to know that Christ had the same problem with his apostles.

One can expect the Pharisees to be a tough audience. They have a personal and professional interest in resisting the message of Jesus. Their position is understandable if not forgivable. But what about the apostles who live under Christ's influence on an hourly basis, every day, month after month? He treats them well. He explains matters patiently. He loves them. He practices what he preaches. There is no contradiction between what he says and what he does. Yet his apostles still miss the point of who he is and what he is doing.

Worried about them and frustrated, he tells them they should not absorb the "leaven of Herod and the Pharisees." Leaven is the yeast that makes bread dough rise. Usually, it has this positive connotation. Jesus gives it a negative slant. Herod's corruption and the Pharisees' hypocrisy are a poisoning leaven for the faith of God's people. They have become pure secularists.

Jesus tells his dear apostles they are affected by that secular virus and they should notice it. Instead of listening to what he was saying, they grumble among themselves about a bread shortage in their kitchen supplies. Every stymied parent and teacher can see the look on Christ's face as he ponders their incomprehension. If Jesus ever yelled at his apostles, it might have been at this time. It was like hitting the donkey over the head with a board to get its attention. Jesus peppered them with seven questions designed to wake them up:

Why do you talk about having no bread?

Are your hearts so hardened you do not understand?

Do you not see with your eyes or hear with your ears?

Do you not remember the first bread miracle?

How many baskets did you collect from the leftovers?

How many baskets of leftovers from the second miracle?

Do you not yet understand? (cf. 17-21).

Mark's text drops the conversation there, much as a parent and teacher would let the matter go, hoping that one day the light will dawn.

Jesus did not let the resistance of the Pharisees nor the slow learning curve of the apostles arrest his mission. At Bethsaida he cured a blind man. As in the case of the deaf man, Jesus gave the blind man special personal attention. He took him by the hand to a private place outside the village. He used spittle because of the popular belief that it had curative qualities. He laid his hand on the man's eyes.

Jesus began with the culture of the man and used the physical signs familiar to the blind one. We know Jesus could cure simply with a word, or even with no word as when the woman with the issue of blood touched him. But Jesus took the material world seriously. He honored the culture of those with whom he dealt. God's grace can be mediated through physical signs and cultural acts. The church imitates Jesus in this way through the life of the sacraments and her commitment to enculturation in her mission work.

Most miracles happened instantaneously. This one occurred in stages. Since it dealt with coming to sight, it was a symbol of the Christian's faith journey. We all come to insight slowly, yes much as the apostles did, who still smarted from his rebukes.

You Are the Christ (Mk. 8:27-38)

Now at last a light shines in an apostolic brain. The scene is Caesarea Philippi, a city built by the tetrarch Philip who named it after himself and the Roman emperor. At the height of Christ's greatest frustration with the dense blindness of his followers, he experiences a long-awaited breakthrough. This is a turning point in Mark's account. They will recognize Jesus as Messiah. They will hear the first prediction of the passion.

They had dimly sensed something like this all along. Their repeated expressions of awe and wonder revealed their appreciation of his greatness and their hope that in him the prophecies would be fulfilled. They would scarcely have left all and followed him had this not been so. But all that was a vague and ambiguous understanding. Now they expressed faith in his messiahship, though its full meaning would take much time to grasp — a fact that is just as true of all Christians today.

Jesus asked them what popular opinion said about him. They reported that people thought he was a resurrected John the Baptist, Elijah, or some other prophet. He asked them what they thought. Jesus wanted more than an opinion. He wanted the truth. Jesus bluntly asked them for a faith statement. Peter answered, "You are the Christ." Peter thus becomes the first human being to formally recognize Jesus as the Messiah.

Others had done so more indirectly. The Matthew and Luke infancy narratives report that shepherds and magi had recognized something extraordinary about Jesus. Peter is the one who has words for it. He makes the faith statement.

Jesus then made his first prediction of his passion, death, and resurrection. He knew that their faith in him as Messiah would be clouded by what their culture expected. Jesus decided he must immediately begin purifying their faith from false expectations. He was not going to be a spectacular new King David, a romantic knight from the Middle Ages of Jewish history, slaying the Roman dragon and restoring the glory of Solomon.

In plain and unambiguous language he told them that he would suffer, be killed, and rise from the dead. He demythologized any popular conception of messiahship they harbored. That he was right on target became clear when Peter rebuked him for talking that way. Peter believed he was the Messiah, but he needed a more truthful understanding of his belief. Jesus wasted no time. He publicly dressed down Peter for trying to remake him into a cultural messiah.

To make sure they all got the message, he called Peter a Satan, a tempter who would make him conform to a wrongheaded interpretation of messiahship. "You are not on the side of God, but on the side of men." To drive the point home even more forcefully, Jesus proceeded to give a profile of what Christian discipleship is really all about. It demanded self denial, cross carrying and following Christ's own road to suffering, death, and resurrection.

Jesus did not soften his words. He had no more time for the velvet touch. The opposition to him was gathering momentum. His apostles needed to grow up spiritually. Only a mature realism could toughen them for the days ahead. Christian life will have its alleluia moment, but the long haul is self purification and cross carrying.

This was no time for a conservative attitude toward one's life and powers and talents. Caution that protected the self from the energy of giving life to the last drop is not his way. This is what he meant by saving life and thus losing it. Never using life for the grand passion for which it was meant by Christ is to lose it. Only when it was "lost," that is when it was poured out with love and enthusiasm, is life really "gained."

Who remembers the timid who fearfully clutch their love and dole it out sparingly? Who reads about the calculating persons who measure their involvement by the prevailing winds of fashion and culture? Only the heroines, heroes, and saints who have the courage to lose the whole world will gain an even greater goal. Love never triumphs by saving it for a rainy day. Love warms no hearts by being kept in the freezer. Love's excitement comes in the using. Love's exaltation comes in losing even one's life for the cause of salvation and the search for holiness.

The world's rewards are finally like the ashes left in the fireplace after the fire of temporary glory is gone. But the ashes of the martyrs, the Christian disciples and witnesses, are transformed into resurrection and eternal life. Love's victory laughs in the face of death. What point is there in gaining the whole world and losing one's soul? Who will be around to comfort the spiritual loser? Where will be the flatterers and sycophants and hangers-on? Of what use is the fickle praise of the public when a lifetime of effort goes up in the fatuous smoke of a life never given to love as Christ meant love to be?

Such was the crescendo of Christ's words to his apostles at the dawn of their first formal recognition of him as Messiah. Gone for the moment was the patient teacher, the mentor who nourished the tender plant through the processes of growth, the wise man who was content to let time work its magic. Jesus believed they were ready for a far more powerful push forward — thus his dazzling set of sayings that dared to uphold persecution, martyrdom, death, suffering, loss of all that had been familiar, a spiritual adventure that laughed at the world's rewards. He was telling them how divine love works in a human context. Never again would he expect anything less of them.

Reflection

1. Does the story of Babette's Feast remind me of other examples of total and conditionless giving?
2. What kinds of social ministry have I engaged in?
3. Do I see the double call to social ministry and spiritual ministry as complementary to one another? Explain.
4. The leaven of Herod and the Pharisees is another way of talking about a purely secular view of life. Are there similar philosophies today? Discuss.
5. Can I sympathize with Christ's frustration at the slowness of the apostles in grasping who he was and what his ministry meant? What are some examples from my own life?
6. What are some false or incomplete views of who Christ is that are held by some people in today's world?
7. How could Peter have faith in Jesus as Messiah and still be so wrong about what this meant?

8. Am I ready to be a disciple of Jesus in the challenging terms he laid out in this chapter?
9. How would I "lose" my life in order to "gain" it?

Prayer

Challenging Lord, you have cared for me tenderly in my faltering stages of faith growth. I know you also want me to grow up and be mature in my faith life. Take my fears away. Give me courage to deny myself, take up my cross, and follow you. Strengthen me, Lord.

9 Christ in Glory

Glory on a Mountaintop (Mk. 9:1-13)

Six days later, Jesus took Peter, James, and John to the top of a mountain where they experienced the mystery of the Transfiguration. Mark does not mention the name of the mountain, but tradition says it happened on Mount Tabor. The Eastern church celebrates this mystery as the feast of Taborion — the Tabor Event. A pilgrimage church crowns this mountain that overlooks the plains of Esdrelon and the little village of Naim where Jesus raised the widow's son from the dead.

Enshrined in the dome is a gold and white mosaic of Christ transfigured in glory. A window in the dome catches the morning sun so that each day Christ still shines like the sun and his clothes are white as snow. Chapels have been erected in honor of Moses and Elijah so that the wish of Peter that "tents" be built for them has been fulfilled. The vision confirmed the revelation of Christ's messiaship at Caesarea Philippi and introduced them to the revelation of Christ as Son of God.

Coming so soon after Christ's teaching about the cross, the Transfiguration put into perspective what must have been a devastating shakeup of their understanding about who the real Messiah was. Surpassing glory lay beyond the humiliations of the passion. This great vision on the mount would also be for every Christian a promise of the kind of transformation that all believers would receive. All Christians will share in the glory that blazed out in Jesus. The just will shine like the sun in the Kingdom of God. St. Paul would teach the same message, assuring us that the sufferings of the present time cannot be compared to the glory that will be revealed in each of us.

Moses and Elijah appeared with Jesus. Moses represented the

law, the Torah of God, that guided every believer into an active and loving relationship with God. Elijah stood for all the prophets who brought people back to the covenant when they had strayed from God's law. Thus the two greatest religious leaders of the Old Testament and the three major apostles of the New Testament witnessed this special revelation of Jesus Christ.

These five witnesses are the trumpets of the two testaments resounding in harmony their music about one eternal Word of God. Ancient prophecy and Gospel teaching sing with one voice the praise of Christ. The stained glass windows of Chartres cathedral catch this sense of biblical unity when they depict the apostles sitting on the shoulders of the prophets. Christ in glory is their colorful focus.

The radiance of the Transfiguration provides a clear and unmistakable principle for understanding Scripture in which the shadows of the law and the prophets contain the mystery of Christ revealed now in the sunlight and reality of the new covenant. Jesus embodies the full truth spoken by the prophets and joyously gives the grace needed to obey in faith the interior attitudes that make the law of God the road to salvation. Never had Jesus seemed to them more evidently the joy of human desiring.

A cloud rested on them and the voice of God said, "This is my beloved Son. Listen to him" (verse 7). Saint Thomas Aquinas says this scene recalls the baptism of Jesus. We paraphrase here his comparison of the two events. At the Jordan, the Father spoke of his Son and the Spirit hovered like a dove over Jesus. That was the visible beginning of the process by which the Holy Trinity inaugurated our salvation.

At Mount Tabor, the Trinity again is present for what is a sign of the ultimate fulfillment of salvation in the resurrection of Christ. The Father is present in the voice. The Spirit comes in the radiant cloud. The Son is present in Jesus. In our baptism the Holy Spirit confers a new innocence as symbolized by the dove. In our resurrection the Spirit will liberate us into a permanent delivery from evil as symbolized by the purity and freshness of the bright cloud.

As they came down the mountain, Jesus warned them not to talk about this to anyone until he had risen from the dead. Talk about "revelation overload!" (no disrespect intended). A few weeks before,

Jesus had scolded them about not grasping the meaning of the Bread miracles. Now they had to absorb the revelations of his messiahship, his suffering and death — plus his Easter glory, so vividly disclosed to them at Tabor. All this so suddenly!

Only subsequent events, their experiences of the tragedy of the passion, the joy of Easter, and the dynamic power received from the Spirit at Pentecost, would make all this clear. An insight does not reveal all its meaning and implications right away.

Does a wedding couple realize all the implications of the sweet vows they pronounce on their wedding day? Did Einstein envision right away what his theory of relativity would mean for the world? Could Henry Ford have imagined the traffic jams his car assembly line concept would one day produce? All the insights were true. Only time reveals what the insights will accomplish.

The deeper the insight, the greater will be the process for appreciating it. Jesus is giving them bread for the painful journey ahead. Somehow it will sustain them when all seems lost. Gradually, they will have an awakening that brings them back to these events and gives them the capacity to explain and apply these explanations to Christian life.

One last comment about insight and the depth of a revelation. The apostles over a long period of time have been accumulating a number of special experiences of Christ. They have witnessed numerous miracles and heard him preach many times. They have received private teachings from him. They have watched him pray. Jesus has related to them in the countless ways that close companionship brings about. They have felt the power of his personal presence day after day. Jesus provided them with an environment that made their faith possible. He formed them into a community. He informed them on many issues. Little by little he transformed the apostles in a way that prepared them for the insights that now flood their awareness. Jesus created in them the readiness that made all that possible.

Now that they have professed their faith in Christ's messiaship, a troubling problem bothered them. The scribes taught that Elijah would come to herald the Messiah's triumph. They based their teaching on the third chapter of Malachi. Popular piety claimed that Elijah would appear exactly three days before the revelation of the Messiah.

It was as if they said, "Well, you are here. What happened to Elijah?" Jesus says that Elijah has come. Most commentators teach that Jesus is referring to John the Baptist.

Like Elijah-John the Baptist, Jesus will suffer much before rising from the dead.

The Power of Faith (Mk. 9:13-29)

The good news about mountaintop experiences is that they make people feel so good. The bad news is that one must come down from the mountain and back to ordinary life. The glory of the mountain is meant to help one to minister in the shadows. The inspiration from the mountain provides energy to shepherd people in the valley.

The warm feelings from the mountain dispersed quickly when they rejoined their companions who were arguing with some scribes. Immediately, a man came up to Jesus to tell him about his epileptic son. A speechless spirit throws him on the ground, where he foams at the mouth, grinds his teeth and then lies there rigid. The boy's father had asked the disciples to cure him but they were unable.

A surge of disappointment and impatience momentarily depressed Jesus and he exclaimed, "O faithless generation, how long am I to be with you?" (verse 19). The frustrated emotions that he vented on the apostles after the Bread miracles he now lets loose on everyone. His dark anger seemed all the more sharp after the ecstasy on the mountain. At the same time, he never let his feelings get in the way of what had to be done. Jesus was not given to self pity. He came to give pity to others. He let people honestly know how he felt and then faced the demands of life as they came to him.

Looking at the distressed father, Jesus asked some questions about the boy's case history. The father told him that a spirit has possessed his son since childhood, sometimes even throwing him into a roaring fire or the river to destroy him. Pleadingly, he asked Jesus to do something, if he is able. Sadly, the failure of the disciples put some doubt in the man's mind about Christ's capacity to help. Just as unfortunately today, the failures of Christian ministers to be caring and compassionate people make outsiders doubt the credibility of Jesus for modern society.

Jesus had just voiced his judgement about a faithless generation, so now he must awaken this man's faith or there will be no cure. Happily, he found a responsive man, whose answer deserves to be a daily prayer on the lips of all Christians. "I do believe, help my unbelief!" (verse 24). Jesus then exorcised the demon from the young man. After convulsing him terribly, the spirit left him so limp he seemed to be dead. The scene of Jesus taking him by the hand and raising him up is like a resurrection image, very appropriate in the light of the mystery of the Transfiguration only moments before.

Later, the embarrassed disciples asked Jesus why they could not exorcise the boy. Jesus told them that they needed much more prayer power before they could exorcise such a spirit. Some ancient texts, though less authoritative, state that Jesus told them they needed fasting as well as prayer for this act. In any event, it was clear to them that they must be filled with divine power if they are going to be effective in this ministry.

Second Prophecy of the Passion and Resurrection (Mk.9:30-32)

The Galilean ministry was coming to a close. Jerusalem and the passion loomed ahead. Jesus took the apostles away from the crowds. Before the forthcoming upheaval, the disciples needed intensive instruction and catechesis. At the top of the agenda is Christ's passion and resurrection. In this second prediction, Jesus used the expression "handed over" to indicate that he will be betrayed. He knew now that one of the twelve would never come to faith in him.

Mark says they did not understand him and were afraid to ask him. They surely understood that he was in deep trouble with the religious authorities. They had heard rumors about steps being taken against him and they had seen the angry faces of his enemies. When he said he would be killed, that was not beyond their imagining. What they did not understand was his prediction of the resurrection. They knew what the words meant, but could not envision how such a thing could occur.

Even the chosen three — Peter, James, and John — who had beheld Christ's glory on the mountain did not understand Jesus' words of resurrection. They had the insight but did not know where to go with it. It seemed incredible, too good to be true. They all were afraid to ask him about it. Denial and avoidance are typical human traits. They were not ready to come to terms with the resurrection of the body. Even when Jesus actually rose from the dead, they could hardly believe it at first. We contemporary Christians often have the same problem. We know what Jesus said and did, but somehow we are not quite ready to live by his teachings.

Jesus Catechizes the Apostles (Mk. 9:33-49)

The group settled in at Peter's home in Capernaum for continued discussion and catechesis. Noticing that several of them were having a hot discussion on the trip to Capernaum, Jesus asked them what was bothering them. Ashamed to tell him, they were silent, each waiting for the other to speak up. Having heard some snatches of their lively debate, Jesus concluded they were again talking about power and position. Who was the greatest among them? Ever looking for a vivid way to put across his point, he asked one of the children in the household (it could have been Peter's little niece) to come and stand in their midst.

He gave them time to feel their fatherly attitudes toward this little child and to experience her innocence. While they were charmed by this scene, Jesus taught them that the greatest person among them is one who serves. If authority is not an authority of service then it is a sign that the person lacks greatness. In that paternalistic culture, where strong authoritarians ruled the roost, his words were as counter-cultural as you could get. Then lifting up the smiling child, he told them how to acquire the attitude of greatness. Just as a child looks at the world with fresh, untainted eyes, so must they be childlike, and that will open them to his teaching about greatness.

Adding a second lesson, Jesus indicated that a child has no power. A child is on the receiving end of things. The apostles' ministry will be to serve the needs of the world's children and those whom they represent — the poor, the oppressed, the hungry, the unjustly treated. Whoever serves the needy of the world, serves Christ and the Father who sent him. That is what will really make people great. To serve others is to be great.

John asked Jesus a question about someone who was exorcising demons in Christ's name. Since this person was not a follower of Jesus, the apostles tried to stop him. Popular exorcisms usually included the invocation of a name more powerful than the demon. The fame of Christ's power led this man to be a successful exorcist. This incident prompted Jesus to offer a lesson in tolerance. Let the exorcist alone. If he can do mighty works in Christ's name, he will not speak ill of him. A person who is not against us is for us. If an act is good and loving, everyone benefits.

Once more pointing to the child, Jesus sternly warned them about scandal being given to the little ones of the world. Better to hang a millstone around one's neck and be drowned. These heavy stones were used for grinding grain and were sometimes used for executions by drowning. Jesus drove home the point about a sinful life that causes others to sin and to lose their souls.

Better to cut off the hand that causes sin, than to have two hands in the unquenchable fire. Better to cut off the foot that produces sin than to have two feet in Gehenna. This was a large garbage dump south of Jerusalem. In ancient times, human sacrifices were offered there to Molech. Its fires and sour smelling smoke symbolized the torment meant for the damned. Better to pluck out the eye that led one into sin than to have two eyes in hell.

Jesus is not calling for literal physical mutilation. His strong words and powerful images were meant to reveal how much he hated sin and what it did to damn the people who refused salvation and even led others into that path by scandalizing them.

The Image of Salt (Mk. 9:49-50)

Christ's three sayings about salt are collected here into one place. Each saying has a different meaning, the only connection being the image of salt. The apostles will need to be salted with fire. Priests salted the sacrificial animals to make them acceptable to God. The apostles must expect to be tried by the fire of suffering as an essential part of being a disciple of Christ. Then they can become the salt of the earth, ministers who witness the taste and purity of the Gospel. Finally, they should practice the salt of hospitality, be at peace with each other and forget about power and position.

Reflection

1. What images help me to appreciate Christ in glory?
2. What are some spiritual transformation stories I could share with others?
3. Why is the Transfiguration such a clear way of understanding the unity of the Old and New Testaments?
4. Elijah is prominent in the Transfiguration story. He appears in the vision. The apostles bring him up in the discussion afterwards. Why is Elijah so important to them?
5. Why were the disciples unable to exorcise the epileptic boy?
6. The apostles did not understand Christ's prophecy about his resurrection. They were even afraid to talk to him about it. What are some personal situations in my life that scare me and prevent me from asking questions about them?
7. The overwhelming message of Jesus is a positive one about love, forgiveness, and salvation. Why is Jesus so strong, then, on the question of sin and the bad results of scandal?
8. What are some stories of tolerance from my experience?
9. Have I ever been scandalized? Have I scandalized others?
10. How can I be the salt of the earth?

Prayer

Christ of glory, I worship you and sing the praises of your beauty. In many ways I have felt your love. In the Transfiguration I see your love and realize how utterly magnificent is the beauty of your interest in me and in every human being. I pray that your love will transform me and transfigure my heart into one of purest love.

10 One Flesh and the Needle's Eye

Marriage and Children (Mk. 10:1-16)

The Galilean ministry is done.

Jesus began his Judean mission with a teaching on the permanence of the marriage bond. He based his words on the text of Genesis 2:24 about Adam and Eve being two in one body. Following Christ's lead, a meditation on the role of the body in the creation story fits well here. These thoughts are based on Pope John Paul II's sermons on the creation stories.

How did Adam know he was different from plants and animals? His body told him. He could see the difference. His body was a communications medium, a built-in microphone. Aristotle taught that whatever is in the mind was first in the senses or the body. Adam learned a lot from his body. Its goodness and holiness told him about the loving graciousness of God the creator. The best message he received from his body is that he was an image of God.

The body let him know he was alone. Not lonely, because he had not experienced another human being. He could not miss what he never had. His original solitude was the first retreat. Humanity began in contemplation. His solitude helped him discover his identity and mission, like naming animals and taking care of the garden.

God did not want the first man to be always alone because such a human is incomplete. Who is missing? A woman. Her body would also tell her the human difference from plants and animals, the feeling of goodness and holiness, and being an image of God. When Adam saw her body, he experienced his difference as a male. When Eve saw his body, she identified herself as a woman. They noticed they complemented each other. Together, they felt more human.

Genesis says they were "naked, but not ashamed" (2:25). They were comfortable with their bodies that gave them no cause for shame. In that original time, shame of the nude body did not exist because neither person had the disordered passions which might induce fear, guilt, or shame. They beheld the pure goodness and value of their bodies and sexuality as God intended them to. Nothing disturbed their intimate gaze on each other. They realized they were God's gifts to each other.

Through their bodies they communicated and communed with each other. That is why the Bible used the term "to know" to refer to sexual relations. The woman will speak both of conceiving a child as well as conceiving an idea. Each noticed the other was an image of God. Each provided the other with a richer experience of self. Mutual communion, via their naked and unashamed bodies, made that possible.

Next they discovered the marital meaning of their bodies. They discovered marriage. The husband clings to his wife and the two become one body. Becoming one body in marriage is a bond blessed by God first of all to enable man and woman to know more about the wonders of being human and being God's image. Their sexual act is a message about original unity and tells them a lot about being male and female. Man and woman made a decision to marry — at the invitation of God. They chose a permanent bond based on love and unity.

God blessed them, saying, "Be fertile and multiply" (Gn. 1:28). God intended they should have sex and produce children, thus introducing a new wonder into their bond of love. "The man had relations with his wife, and she conceived, saying, 'I have produced a man with the help of the Lord' " (Gn. 4:1). Hence they experienced the generativity of their bodies. With divine help they produced a new image of God.

What lessons do we learn from original time, the "beginning?"
— That the body is a teacher.
— That the body reveals our differences from other creatures and our identity with the image of God.
— That, due to God's will, the body discloses goodness and holiness. It was not meant to be a source of shame. Shame was the result of sin and it led to disordered passion.
— That God willed the goodness of sexuality within marriage.

— That the bodies of man and woman complement each other, revealing a fuller sense of humanity and providing the possibility of the joy of love and communion.

— That the conjugal union of man and woman should make them one body in a permanent and indissoluble union.

— That the couple is called to parenthood and the nurturing of children.

These reflections offer the backdrop to Christ's reply to the Pharisees' question about divorce. Did he think it was lawful? He asked them what Moses taught. They replied that Moses allowed a certificate of divorce. Jesus answered that Moses did that because of the hardness of people's hearts, but "In the beginning, it was not so" (verse 6). Jesus took his listeners back to the beginning, where divorce was not envisioned in God's plan for creation.

Jesus lifted his listeners above their preoccupation with reasons for divorce to contemplate God's purpose for marriage. Taking them away from the problems of the present — Herod's divorce and the religious grounds for divorce — back to original time, he showed them God's own plan for love and marriage. He became their tour guide to the pre-history of the world, a time when the purity of God's purposes started everything. Before the Fall, the divinely appointed cultural ideal is unity and love. Man and woman, in conjugal union, rediscover each time the mystery of creation. They call each other by name and so reveal to one another that their greatness is always in communion with each other. "What, therefore, God has joined together, let no man put asunder" (verse 9).

Later, when they were alone, the apostles asked Jesus again about his teaching on marriage and divorce. Jesus said plainly that a spouse — man or woman — who divorces and remarries is committing adultery. This was yet another way of teaching them and us the indissolubility of marriage.

Christ's teaching applies to everyone in all times. It is meant for those today who teach that it is too difficult, indeed impossible, to be bound to one person for the whole of life. Jesus' words speak to those in our own culture who reject indissolubility of marriage — and even make fun of the idea. At the same time this teaching does not preclude pastoral care for the separated, divorced, and remarried (cf. Pope John Paul II, *Familiaris Consortio*, Christian Family, #84).

Very fittingly, after this session on marriage, Jesus meets and blesses children brought to him by a host of parents. But the apostles had become protective of Jesus. Gone were the free, light-hearted days of the early Galilean mission tours. Danger and death talk polluted the air. Every encounter raised the tension level and persuaded the apostles to tighten access to Christ.

Generally, Jesus accepted their caution except in the case of children. When they tried to keep the kids away from him, he displayed acute annoyance. Faced with a sea of adult suffering and a tempest of religious opposition, he welcomed renewing contact with the one group of human beings who best reflected what his Gospel attitude was like. He hungered for their laughter, playfulness, and innocence. "Of such is the kingdom of heaven" (verse 14).

He heard the voices of children on the hillsides. Their laughter brought peace to his heart. Here were humans who still possessed some of the qualities he had just spoken about in his reference to original time. What scene on the eve of the passion of Christ could be more affecting than Mark's description of Jesus eagerly hugging the kids and blessing them? They were his best ambassadors about how to accept the Gospel with an open, simple, and trusting attitude.

A Rich Man and Poverty of Spirit (Mk. 10:17-31)

After the young children came a young man, running up to Jesus and kneeling before him. He called Jesus, "Good Teacher" and asked what he needed to do to gain eternal life. Jesus first reminded him that the title "Good" belonged to God alone. Citing six of the commandments, Jesus offered these as the paths to eternal life.

In his Sermon on the Mount, Jesus had delivered a lengthy series of statements on how the commandments were to be properly understood and practiced. He revealed the values they upheld, the attitudes they fostered, and the human happiness they produced — both on earth and in eternity. He could have quoted the psalms. "How shall a young man be faultless in his way? By keeping God's words" (Ps. 119:9).

The young man seemed to want something more. He had observed the commandments all his life. Jesus looked at him with affection. He used the language of "apostle making" to this fine youth. This young man might have become the thirteenth apostle. Jesus already knew that one of the twelve would betray him and may have been thinking of the future replacement that might be needed in the apostolic community. The apostolic call included leaving all and following Jesus.

Probably none of the apostles whom Jesus called had been rich, but neither had they been impoverished. Matthew had funds from his tax collecting business. The fishermen had small, but prosperous businesses. They had families. Proportionate to their states in life, they had a lot to give up. They did so and followed Christ. This rich young man had "great possessions." Jesus had offered him the option for love. Such love was the purpose of the commandments. This love would create a freedom in this man that riches could never supply.

Centuries later, Christ would make the same call to Francis, the rich young man of Assisi, and would hear a magnificent "yes" in response. The depth of Christ's heart reached out to the depth of the heart of this man. Jesus wished he had heard these words. "Within my heart I treasure your promise. With all my heart I seek you" (Ps. 119:10-11). Sadly, the young man's face fell. He could not let go of his wealth. He did not take up Christ's option for absolute love. He was the only one in the gospels to refuse Christ's call to discipleship when it was offered.

Well aware that wealth can come between a person and commitment to him, Jesus twice comments on the problem wealth presents for people. He then used his famous "eye of the needle" image, which stated that it was harder for a rich person to enter the kingdom of heaven than for a camel to go through the eye of a needle. Some people have seen in this image a gate in Jerusalem, called the eye of the needle, so low that a camel cannot walk through it.

Others stay with Christ's image just as he used it, noting that he purposely coined this wild metaphor to dramatize how truly difficult attachment to wealth, on the part of some, can blind them to the proper role of riches. If God has blessed someone with money, God expects the person to be a steward of the money for the good of the world. The kingdom of God, in its earthly expression, is meant to be a community of justice and conscience.

The kingdom use of wealth is meant to minister to the needs of the poor, both to alleviate their immediate suffering and to help society create structures of justice which help the poor find a decent way of life. Just as God has given the whole human race the responsibility to be wise stewards of the earth, the Lord expects the prosperous to be wise stewards of their funds on behalf of the deprived. In kingdom of heaven terms, wealth brings with it moral responsibilities.

Throughout Christian history, many women and men have responded to Christ's call, not just in the stewardship sense, but also in the radical sense. Like Francis of Assisi, they left all and followed Jesus. Sometimes they were rich young women and men, often they were people of ordinary means, or those with nothing at all. The point is, they heard the option for consecrated love and accepted that. Possessions and attachments did not stand in their way. They were touched by love and lost all their fears.

Possibly in a tone of self congratulations, Peter reminded Jesus that he and the apostles (not like the rich young man) had left all and followed him. Implied in his statement was the question about what reward they could expect. Jesus replied that all who do so for the sake of the kingdom of heaven will receive a hundredfold here (including persecution) and eternal life hereafter.

If the apostles become as empty as possible then God can fill them. God cannot force love into a heart. It will be their responsibility to keep emptying their souls even of the yearning for the possessions and attachments they left behind. Their hundredfold is the divine love that will replace the emptiness they have created. It is the pleasure of sharing this love with a world that hungers so much for it.

The more room they make for love, the more divine affection they will receive. The Holy Spirit will fill them with gifts of joy, peace, hope, and meaning to replace attitudes that went with possessiveness. Thus the last — those who have done the most self emptying — will be first. And the first — those who cannot let go — will be last.

Third Prophecy of Passion and Resurrection and Ambition (Mk. 10:32-45)

On the road to Jerusalem, city of the Passion, Jesus delivered his third prediction of his suffering, death, and resurrection. Mark says he walked ahead of them, seemingly at a quicker pace, eager to face the destiny he was describing. Jesus grew more specific this time, noting that he would be mocked, spit upon, scourged, and then killed.

This both amazed and scared the apostles. His message was sinking in and they began to accept the inevitable, though they still could not see why he so resolutely marched toward it. They did not make the connection between the cross of Christ and the salvation of the world. They heard the words. They did not surrender to their real meaning. Nor would they grasp this until after it was all over.

James and John proved this lack of understanding by asking Jesus for prominent places next to him when he entered his glory. Patiently, Jesus told them they did not understand what they asked. They still had power fantasies. He had not been able to shake the David dream from their messianic expectations. They still hungered for a new romantic, poet, warrior king like David to come and be their messiah. They did not understand the essentially spiritual type of messiah that Jesus represented. He asked them if they could drink the cup and go through the baptism. Jesus referred to the cup of suffering and a baptism of fire.

They said they were prepared to accept suffering, but it is doubtful they meant more than being tough men in the difficult days ahead. Peter would show similar bravado. Jesus realized they still missed his point, but noted that one day they would accept the punishing role of discipleship when they were more aware and ready to rely on Christ. He promised them no glory seats. Only the Father did that. The other apostles heard of the brothers' bold request and were mad about it. Jesus used the occasion once again to teach them about true greatness which is related to servanthood.

The Blind Man of Jericho (Mk. 10:46-62)

Having chipped away a little more at the blindness of his

apostles, Jesus must have found it refreshing to deal with the relatively simple matter of curing the physical blindness of the man from Jericho. The traveling group is now only fifteen miles from Jerusalem. Crowds of pilgrims are on their way to the Holy City to celebrate the Passover.

A blind man, named Bartimaeus, heard of the presence of Jesus and yelled for his attention. He asked for mercy. People tried to shut him up. That simply made Bartimaeus bolder, even calling Jesus by the messianic title, Son of David, the very title Jesus normally tried to suppress because of its militaristic and political associations. Jesus summoned the man, who quickly threw off his cloak and rushed to Christ. Jesus asked him what he wanted and Bartimaeus promptly asked for sight. Jesus cured him, noting the solidity of the man's faith. Jesus said he could go back to his own life. But instead Bartimaeus followed him as a disciple.

Bartimaeus gives us a profile of a follower of Christ.

He was aggressive in wanting a face to face encounter with Jesus. He did not have a wistful desire, but an energizing motivation. When Jesus called him, his face did not fall like the rich young man. Bartimaeus threw away the one poor cloak he had and rushed into the presence of Jesus. This was the opportunity of a lifetime and he would not miss it.

He was specific about his needs. He was not indirect, diffident. He knew what he wanted and said so. He called Jesus Son of David in the very mistaken sense that Jesus wanted to efface. But Jesus was not too worried about this blind man who had spent months and years in the silent darkness caused by his blindness. Jesus could tell the man had faith. There would be time enough for him to get the correct view of Christ's messiaship. He healed this good and delightful man and let him go. What a pleasure it must have given Christ's heart to see this man spontaneously follow him to Jerusalem, singing God's praises and with a happy heart walking in the footsteps of the Master.

Reflection

1. Why was Christ's response on the divorce question so effective?

2. In what ways does my body communicate to me?
3. In what ways do I see my body as an image of God?
4. What would be the moral result of considering my body as a temple of the Holy Spirit as St. Paul teaches?
5. What do children teach me about real Gospel attitudes?
6. Do I know stories of today's "rich young persons" whose wealth stops them from being stewards of God's gifts? Is such attachment to today's lifestyles a reason why some men and women refuse a vocation to dedicated ministry?
7. Are there still people who cannot understand Christ's teaching about authority and power as means to service? Share some stories about this.
8. If I were following Jesus as closely as the apostles did, would I have been every bit as unsure about his predictions of the passion and resurrection as they were? What might make me different?
9. Did Christ's sense of loneliness grow in the face of so much misunderstanding? Could he have done anything about it?
10. What could I learn from Bartimaeus?

Prayer

Jesus, I thank you for my family. Keep before me the vision of the beginning and that plan for unity and love. Take me with you now to Jerusalem where I may share in your passion.

11 Branches of Glory and Temple Cleansing

Welcome Messiah! (Mk. 11:1-11)

Jesus now approached the goal of his ministry, which is our salvation from all that oppresses us, above all from sin. This will happen in Jerusalem, the city of destiny. In Mark's gospel, Jesus has carefully subdued all references to him as Messiah, a fact especially evident in his silencing the testimony of the demons. Jesus wanted people to experience him as a person drawing their hearts to conversion to God. He did not want them to be distracted by false cultural expectations and stereotypes of messiahs.

Jesus had visited Jerusalem many times before but not in the same way he did on Palm Sunday. At last, he would consent to a wildly popular acclaim that acknowledged him as Messiah. His messianic march began on the Mount of Olives. Groves of olive trees carpeted that mount. Symbolically, it was the hill of oil, the substance that was used to anoint kings — and one day, the Messiah. Bethpage and Bethany were villages near the Holy City. The Hebrew prefix "beth" means house. Therefore, Bethpage means house of figs and Bethany means house of dates. Most likely, fig orchards surrounded Bethpage and clusters of date palms bordered Bethany.

Jesus presided over the details of his messianic entry into Jerusalem, just as he would supervise the preparations for the Last Supper a few days later. He purposely selected a young donkey instead of a horse for his mount. When a king rode out to war, he strode a horse. When a king marched into a city in peace, he chose a young donkey. With war fever and resentful rebellion in the air, the people ached for a Messiah as liberator.

By choosing a young donkey, Jesus acted counter-culturally against the prevailing mood and taught the onlookers that the real

Messiah was a man of peace. At least for that one day, his witness worked. The people cut branches from trees (Mark does not mention palms) and waved them in his honor, much as they were accustomed to do in the branch waving ritual at the Feast of Tabernacles. That feast was a celebration of their "tent days" (tabernacle being another word for tent) in the desert when God gave them water from rocks and personally led them with his guiding light in the pillar of fire.

In verses 9-10, we hear the crowds' "Hosanna Prayer." That comes from Psalm 118:25-26. Here "Hosanna" means "Save us." It is not the praise language that it signifies for us, such as in the Holy, Holy, Holy of the Eucharist. In this case it was a liturgical shout used in the festive processions at Tabernacles, and now directed to Christ. All of this indicates that Jesus was momentarily successful in modifying their misunderstandings of messiahship.

The march into Jerusalem was more like a procession of religious pilgrims than a potentially explosive political demonstration. It was closer to the joyous parade of "The Saints Go Marching In" than to the martial strains of "The Battle Hymn of the Republic." Jesus was not leading an armed revolt that would result in killing others. He was the front runner in a paschal procession that would culminate in his redemptive death. He changed a political rally into a gathering of the saints. He transformed the drums of war into the trumpets of peace.

In our own day some extreme forms of Liberation Theology seem to support armed revolt against oppression instead of the Christian route of non-violent change. These people want a militant messiah just as much as those in New Testament times. Christ answers them the same way now as in Gospel times. He still rides the young donkey of peace. He will liberate people by his own suffering — not by inflicting pain and death on others. Jesus does desire human dignity for the poor and he wants society to provide them with the opportunity for a decent way of life.

His salvation will encompass the cause of freedom and social justice. But the method he chose to initiate this process was resolutely spiritual. He never became a politician nor a general, though he defended the legitimate rights of Caesar and healed the servant of a centurion whose faith he loudly admired. Jesus chose the most basic way to heal the world's ills — to save each person from the blindness of sin that causes all other troubles.

Jesus was not merely managing evil, but destroying it at its root. The government and the military strive to contain evil and to manage its excesses. Jesus drove deeper and struck at the cause. A philosopher believes he is a success if he can identify the cause of evil. A savior gets rid of it and supplies us with the same power to do so.

Psychology and sociology identify the symptoms of personal and social distress. Their therapies of compassionate counseling and social engineering heal some of the symptoms and provide persons and communities with the capacity to cope. And that is a commendable achievement. But even as the AA people testify, the best they can hope for is to control the symptoms. Without a doubt all these efforts are admirable and necessary.

Jesus, however, went further and struck at the cause of all human ills, the sinfulness that produces alienation from self, others, and God. Just as much as any behavioral scientist, Jesus wanted to eliminate the symptoms of psychological and social pain. His method probed deeper to the depths of the heart and produced the salvation that would heal the heart itself.

Also, Jesus was sympathetic to those who held social responsibilities. He knew how tough their job was. He seldom spoke harshly or negatively to them. He reserved his anger for religious leaders whose vocation it was to keep people's attention on faith, prayer, and the conversion of the human heart. Jesus appreciated the pragmatic demands made on soldiers and politicians and he understood the speculative vocation of a philosopher. He was less patient with the religious leaders who should contemplate the absolutes of faith, hope, love, and prayer and their relationship to God. Jesus considered the primacy of the spirit to be uppermost. He cursed the fig tree that had only leaves and no figs (verse 14). This enacted parable illustrated Christ's frustration with those who deal with the leaves of symptoms instead of the figs of the absolutes of faith, prayer, and trust.

The Temple Cleansing (Mk. 11:15-25)

The temple occupied a thirty-acre area atop Mount Zion. Surrounded by a stout wall, the temple area was divided into a series of walled courtyards. The court of the Gentiles stood at the entrances. Next came the court of women, then the court of the men and finally the court of the priests. In the priests' courtyard stood the temple itself.

The story of the temple cleansing took place in the court of the Gentiles. The place had become a circus. It was meant to be as holy as the whole thirty acres, but instead it became a noisy gathering of gawking gentile tourists, the turbulent clanking of the money changers and the haggling over the price of the sacrificial doves.

Devout Jews were expected to pay a temple tax that amounted to a day's wages for a working man. Since large numbers of pilgrims came from foreign lands, and since the temple administration demanded local currency, there had to be a money exchange booth. A fee was charged for every exchange. Moreover, the family of the high priest, Annas, held a monopoly on the money exchange.

The dove was the offering of the poor. A dove could be purchased at a relatively cheap price in shops near the temple, but the priests decided whether the dove was suitable for sacrifice and usually rejected the store-bought animals. In the court of the Gentiles they sold doves at twenty five times the market price outside. They succeeded in price gouging the poor because they devised numerous ways to disapprove of pre-purchased doves. Most likely Jesus remembered the look on the faces of Mary and Joseph when they had to dole out so much money from the family finances for a dove when they brought him to the temple for Passover in his twelfth year.

Thus the first impression a pilgrim or tourist would get of the temple was that of a noisy, strident, predatory money machine, rooted in greed. This mocked the sanctity of the temple by treating the poor unjustly, robbing them blind and scandalizing everyone. This was an old problem. Centuries before, Jeremiah had railed against the secularization of the temple, which he argued was meant only to be a house of prayer (Jer. 7:11).

The prophet Malachi, equally distressed, predicted that it would take the Messiah himself to clean up the mess. He would come with a reformer's fire. He would sit down in the temple and cleanse the sons of Levi, that is, the priests (Mal. 3:1-3). Fire does more than treat symptoms. It has a transforming power. Messianic fire changes hearts.

That is exactly what Jesus did. Having publicly entered the Holy City as a real Messiah, he undertook the messianic responsibility to cleanse the temple of greed and exploitation of the poor and return it to its original purpose as an environment of prayer. He came in his role as the holy king who ushered in God's kingdom of love, justice, and mercy.

On Holy Thursday and Good Friday, Jesus would be the priest, the lamb who redeems us by his sacrificial offering. At the temple cleansing, Jesus is the prophet who purifies the church by his courageous moral action.

Christ's prophetic witness warns us to avoid all works of injustice. Certainly the church administration must constantly examine and purify itself. Parish leadership should be fair and responsible in its relationship to its people. Every Catholic has the call to be a witness to fairness and justice.

The parish church should be a house of prayer and reverence. It is more than a meeting hall or a multi-purpose room — even if it may be used as such. It is above all a house of God and an environment of reverence and a doorway to transcendence. There the holy mysteries of salvation of celebrated and major spiritual events in the life of a Catholic take place. The shrines of the saints chronicle the history of holiness in the church. The Stations of the Cross re-awaken the call to discipleship that includes the faith journey of the cross.

The font and the altar encompass the saving actions of Christ in Baptism and the Eucharist. The lectern, shrine of the scriptural Word of God calls us to constant conversion. In the celebration of the Eucharist, we share in the saving work of Jesus in the greatest possible way. Vatican II tells us that, "In the Holy Eucharist is contained the whole spiritual good of the church, namely, Jesus our new Passover" (*Presbyterorum ordinis*, Life of Priests, 5). The parish church is a holy place and meant to be a house of prayer.

St. Paul teaches that the body of each Catholic is a temple of the Holy Spirit. We, too, should be houses of prayer and a worship environment. We must practice "temple maintenance" which includes the physical, emotional, mental and spiritual care of our body-persons. Jesus thought of all these elements in his training of the apostles. Their long walks gave them exercise. Their freedom to express themselves openly kept their emotions up front and healthy. The give and take of their dialogues sharpened their minds. Their regular retreats to quiet places restored their souls.

Peter noticed the withered fig tree. We already saw what the act symbolized. Jesus used the withered fig tree as a dramatic visual to explain the failure of the religious leaders. Since his disciples would be the religious leaders of the future, he wanted them to devote themselves to cultivating the attitudes of absolute faith, hope, love, trust, and prayer in the face of an absolute God.

The absolute side of such attitudes is that they should always be whole-hearted drives. Their relative side refers to the life stage in which a disciple journeys as a child, a teenager, a young adult, a mid-life adult, a senior citizen. Each stage brings a more fully developed person to the human-divine relationship.

But regardless of the stage, absolute surrender is always called for. Jesus was basically saying, "No matter what life stage you are at, you should believe, love, trust, obey, and praise God with ALL your mind (not just part of it), ALL your heart (God does not want a divided heart), and ALL your soul (not a hesitant dedication)."

Jesus knew perfectly well that people spend most of their conscious hours with transient, superficial, symptomatic, relative experiences. Did he not face the same experiences each day? He observed that every day brought dozens of little adjustments, compromises, and practical adaptations. The flow of the finite crowded out the awareness of the absolute.

It does not have to be that way. He does not fear to tell them that they could move mountains with prayer. He asked them to purge all doubt from their hearts. Very likely, the apostles — members of the passionate culture of the Palestine of that day — could really hear a savior posit these absolute challenges.

Our own culture, embedded in the thousand, complex details of modern life, has made a virtue of being tentative, diffident, skeptical, dispassionate, and suspicious of anyone who dares to be absolute about anything. We live in a temperature taking universe. We are forever checking the pulse rate of our moral reactions. Hence it seems perverse to talk about any absolutes.

Nothing should be wholeheartedly embraced. Nonetheless, Christ's absolute challenge to absolute faith, hope, love, and trust in God remains. This is not only possible, but needed more than ever to respond to the fulfillment hungers of people today.

Christ's Authority (Mk. 11:27-33)

Mark shows that Christ had been on a collision course with the religious leaders for a long time. His Palm Sunday celebration and his cleansing of the temple produced an intense challenge to them. He had bearded the lion in his own den, not in some faraway provincial town.

Jesus is not evasive. He does not scale back his position. He does not enter a dialogue with his cards tightly held against his vest. They know exactly where he stands and what he wants. When the religious leaders ask him the source of his authority for these teachings and deeds, he responds by asking them a question. Who was the source of authority for John the Baptist?

If they express their real opinion, namely, that they did not like the baptist and doubted his moral and divinely based authority, they would alienate the people who dearly loved and admired John. If they admit the divine authority of John, then Jesus would ask them why they did not support him. So they chose silence. Jesus told them that he would not let them know the source of his authority, since they would not take a stand on their real beliefs. Jesus refused to compromise his absolute principles and teachings.

Reflection

1. How did Jesus turn the Palm Sunday procession into a religious event?
2. How did Jesus evaluate the social responsibilities of politicians and military leaders?

3. Why is Jesus less patient with religious leaders than with political and military ones?
4. What does it mean to say that Jesus dealt with the causes of evil, while the politicians and the soldiers only managed the symptoms of social evil?
5. Why can it be said that psychology and sociology usually only deal with the emotional and social symptoms of evil and not so much their cause?
6. A philosopher can identify the cause of evil. Where does Jesus differ from a philosopher?
7. What are some examples of temple cleansing needed in our own church? In our own lives?
8. How can I make absolute acts when I am always changing from one life stage to another and am always in a changing society?
9. What is there about my life experience that makes it difficult for me to even think about absolutes?
10. What did Jesus mean when he said we should have a faith that can move mountains?

Prayer

Dear Jesus of the spiritual absolutes, show me how to take my whole mind and focus it on total belief in you. Enlighten my will so that I can totally trust in you. Enlarge my heart so I can love you without reserve. Empower my spiritual strength to the point where I am willing to give all my strength to hoping in you.

12 A Vine, a Tax and a Mite

The Vineyard Parable (Mk. 12:1-12)

Jesus never stopped trying to lead his adversaries to see and accept the truth. He dialogued, witnessed, scolded, and invited them to accept him, his message, and his saving work. In the vineyard parable, he proposed a story as a method for opening them up. Wine making was a major business in Palestine. A typical vineyard was surrounded by stone wall or a thick, tight hedge to keep animals and robbers out. People crushed the grapes with their feet in the winepress, underneath which was a vat to receive the juice. Guards used the lookout tower which also had rooms for the workers. Many vineyards had absentee landlords who prized them as good investments. Often these owners caused unrest and resentment either by their unjust demands or by their impersonal ownership and lack of involvement in the problems of the workplace.

Jesus took this well known situation and applied it to his mission. He updated Isaiah's popular "Song of the Vineyard" (Is. 5:1-7), a story well known in rabbinical preaching on the subject of Israel's perennial infidelity to the covenant. Hence the pertinence of Christ's use of the Isaian parable, for he relied on a familiar religious image in the preaching cycle and cultural image from the wine industry.

Jesus followed the traditional Isaian story line up to a point. God is the owner of the vineyard. Israel is the tenant farmer. The various servants who come to collect the contracted barrels of wine are beaten, wounded, and even killed. These servants are the prophets. Jesus added a new detail about the "beloved son" who should have received better treatment. God had called Jesus "beloved son" at the Jordan baptism and at the Transfiguration, hence it is Jesus who is the beloved son of the story.

The cultural reference does not quite fit the parable. God is the owner, but not an uncaring landlord. The tenant farmers have been given a generous deal and have not been badly treated. The servant-prophets had not cheated or made unfair demands on the farmers as was often the real situation. Hence there is no room for sympathy for an underdog (none existed here). The tenants displayed ingratitude for a generous arrangement. They have harshly broken their covenant contract, even to the point of murdering the only son of the owner.

Christ's second addition to the old story was his remark about the rejection of the stone that would become the future cornerstone of the messianic kingdom. This was an allusion to his resurrection. Some believe the stone image was based on a word play. The Hebrew word "ben" means son. The Hebrew word "eben" means stone. Jesus the "ben" was the "eben."

Jesus used the story to illustrate the judgement that would be imposed on his adversaries, but he also hoped it might open their hearts to conversion. After all they had used the story to preach to others about their infidelity. But when Christ's updated story was applied to them, they lacked the humility and insight to accept it.

Coin of the Realm (Mk. 12:13-17)

The ominous mood of deadly controversy permeates the Marcan account of Holy Week. The series of opposition stories he places in this context prepare us psychologically for the fatal outcome on Good Friday. Such was the debate about taxes, which in every society are a touchy subject. A proverb puts it that death and taxes are the only certainties.

An unholy alliance of strange bedfellows — Pharisees and Herodians — approached Jesus about the explosive tax issue. They buttered him up with flattering comments about his moral integrity and courageous frankness, a slimy beginning since their real sentiments were exactly the opposite. They hoped to force Christ into a no-win situation. Asking him if it was all right to pay taxes to Caesar, they knew he would arouse public anger if he said yes. People hated Roman taxation. If he opposed the taxes he risked government wrath and possible arrest.

Christ first disposed of their duplicity. They were not honestly looking for a solution to an ethical question. They wanted to eliminate a troublesome prophet. By asking them why they asked him such a question, he let them know he was onto their real game. But he did not retreat in grumpy silence and avoid the issue. The occasion gave him a chance to enunciate one of his best known statements about religion and society.

Good teacher that he was, he used a familiar visual to make his point. Holding up a Roman coin, he drew their attention to the image of Caesar and said, "Repay to Caesar what belongs to Caesar and to God what belongs to God" (verse 17). This teaching has been used to justify the legitimate separation of church and state, but it may not be employed to justify the separation of the church and society.

Popes, bishops, and priests uphold and teach those Gospel norms which are helpful for a just and peaceful society. It is the duty of all God's people, especially the laity, to minister to and influence society and even the government with these Gospel values. The ordained minister to the baptized's needs for holiness, love, mercy, and forgiveness. In turn the baptized carry this mission to society and government.

St. Jerome applied this saying of Christ also to the image that is on the "coin of the soul." This is God's image on our spiritual coinage. We are to render to God the faith, hope, love, and trust that is required on our side of our relationship to God.

Who is the Real Husband? (Mk. 12:18-27)

The Sadducees did not believe in immortality. Rich and elite, most of them were priests. They considered the pentateuch (the first five books of the Bible) to be the most authoritative scriptural texts. Hence the books of the prophets and Wisdom were thought to be of secondary importance. The Sadducees judged that no text in the pentateuch supported belief in immortality.

In fact, the Sadducees chose a teaching about the Levirate law from the pentateuch to demonstrate how absurd the immortality position was. The law prescribed that a brother should marry his deceased brother's widow — who as yet had no children — to assure the continuity of the family line and conserve the family property (Dt. 25:5-6). The Sadducees illustrated this law with an extreme (some might even say ridiculous) example. Seven brothers marry one woman. Each brother died, leaving the woman without issue. Who then is the real husband in heaven?

Jesus gave them a two level response. First, the future life is different from the present one insofar as we will become spiritual like the angels in the next life and there will not be marriage in the physical, sexual sense. Secondly, Jesus took the Burning Bush story to argue in favor of immortality (Ex. 3:2,6). When Moses asked God who he was, God responded the famous identification, "I am who am." But God also said to Moses that he was the God of Abraham, Isaac, and Jacob. Jesus then noted that they all believed that God was the Lord of the living and not of the dead. Everyone knew that the patriarchs died. But if God is still their Lord, they must be alive in a new existence. Immortality must be a truth.

In our present secularized culture, belief in immortality has eroded among those whose lives are caught up in sex and affluence. Many psychologists have noted that people subconsciously immerse themselves in sex as a method for staving off death. Probably, this arises from the nature of sex as a means for producing life. But these people do not want babies. They want to deny death. Such an attitude implicitly denies immortality.

Affluence causes many to be absorbed in material interests and addictively possessive about this world's assets. This makes them tone deaf about the message of immortality. A tone deaf person cannot hear the melody. A spiritually tone deaf person cannot hear the music of immortality. Interestingly enough, the Sadducees belong to the affluent members of their society. Did that close them to immortality? They used a sex-related argument to deny immortality. Were they also afflicted with the subconscious belief that sex helped them stave off death? No answer can be given. We can with greater confidence state that excessive preoccupation with sex and affluence in modern culture dulls the sensitivity to a future life and immortality.

The Command to Love (Mk. 12:28-34)

It is popularly thought that the Old Testament is about cold justice and the New Testament deals with the warmth of love. Jesus dispelled this myth in his conversation with a religious leader, who was a sincere searcher for truth and an honest admirer of Christ. The scribe asked Jesus which was the greatest commandment. Jesus replied by quoting from a text about the love of God (Dt. 6:4) and one about the love of self and neighbor (Lv. 19:18).

These two commandments which seem so "Christian" were actually quite Jewish and imbedded in the heart of the Old Testament. Still, there is no arguing that Christians have taken these love rules to their hearts and consider them to be the highest of Christian ideals and callings. It is equally true that all Christians must confess they have as difficult a time as anyone living up to such demanding invitations to love.

The scribe was impressed with Christ's responses. He repeated the teachings of Jesus and added words about the sublime unity of God and the superiority of love to burnt offerings and sacrifices. Jesus could not have said it better and expressed his admiration for the scribe, whom he said was not far from the kingdom of God.

Scribes and Mites (Mk. 12:35-44)

Jesus then gave a teaching about true messiahship. He asked his listeners why David called the Messiah Lord, if the Messiah was really a son of David. Jesus was giving a commentary on Psalm 101:1. David sings, "The Lord (God) said to my Lord (the Messiah) . . ." Jesus explained that the real Messiah was more than a genealogical son of David, destined (as they thought) to repeat the glamorous military exploits of his famed ancestor. The Messiah was to be a king of peace and the author of the spiritual kingdom of God.

As always Jesus saved his toughest talk for those in charge of religion. This time he took on the scribes and criticized their pretentiousness, wearing long robes, expecting special public acknowledgements, taking the best seats in the synagogues, and honored places at feasts.

He had just said that they devour widows' inheritances when he saw a poor widow put a mite into the temple treasury which had thirteen trumpet shaped collection boxes. Each one had a special purpose, one for oil, one for corn, one for wine, and so on. Rich people were putting in large sums. The widow put in two mites, a word that literally means a thin coin, worth one fortieth of one pence.

Jesus drew his disciples' attention to her humble offering. He told them that the rich were giving from their abundance, but this poor lady gave from her substance. The rich had plenty of money left. The poor widow gave all she had. He used the experience to teach them about sacrificial giving. She had given more than the rich. He was basically saying that generosity means giving until it hurts. He held up the best example of generosity he could find, a poor widow who gave the equivalent of one tenth of a penny.

Mother Teresa is fond of saying that God does not expect great deeds of us. God only wants small deeds done with great love. It is the interior drive of the soul that truly measures the quality of our acts. Jesus had just taught the greatest commandments. He delighted in finding a widow who illustrated exactly what he was getting at in inviting us to put our whole energy of love behind every act of ours.

Reflection

1. God has given us the vineyard of our personal selves. He expects good and abundant fruit to appear. How have I cultivated and shared the fruits of my person?
2. In what sense might I have beaten off, even killed God's servants who come to harvest the good fruit expected of our lives?
3. Have I in any way ever snuffed out the "beloved son" who wished to draw from me the fruits of love for the good of the world?
4. What are some examples of Church-state conflict in our society?
5. What are some examples of Church-society conflict in our world?
6. What is the difference between the responsibilities of the ordained and the baptized?
7. How can I tell whether there is practical belief in immortality in our world?
8. What would I think of someone who wants to help the poor by

saying, "We should not promise them heaven hereafter. We must work to give them a decent way of life here on earth."

9. How could I prove to someone that love was a central commandment of the Old Testament?

10. What are some motivations for sacrificial giving?

Prayer

Beloved Son, you suffered rejection and death at the hands of the tenants of the vineyard. I am a tenant, farming the vineyard of my personhood and the world you have entrusted to me. Give me the attitudes of love of God, self, and others along with true sacrificial giving so that I may joyfully yield the fruits of peace, harmony, and community which you expect of me.

13   Judge of the Living and the Dead

This chapter is difficult to understand. Mainly, Jesus talks about the end of world and the second coming. We affirm this in the Nicene Creed when we say, "He will come again in glory to judge the living and the dead." Christ used images familiar to his listeners, but strange to us. He took the teachings of the prophets about the Day of the Lord to comment on problems that lay ahead for his disciples and the Last Judgement as well.

Jewish religious thinkers believed that God would give the chosen people a world in which God's rule would be perfectly realized. They believed that such a kingdom could not be made out of the sinful world they beheld. God would have to destroy this world and transform it into the new kingdom. This would happen on the Day of the Lord. The change would be violent, hence they chose catastrophe language to describe it. This language was called apocalyptic, or revelation talk. It has a dreamlike and visionary quality to it. Stars fall. The sun darkens and the moon gives no light. Evil omens, such as false prophets, abound.

Jesus used this language and the theme of the day of the Lord to teach several truths. (1) The Temple and the city of Jerusalem will be destroyed. (2) His disciples can expect persecution. (3) This world will come to an end eventually and then the Second Coming will take place. (4) His disciples should prepare for these events.

Jesus mixed these themes together, letting one serve as a symbol of the other. The destruction of the temple and Jerusalem is an image of the final end of the world. It is also a sign of the birthpangs of the emergence of the Christian church in which the disciples can expect suffering as part of this process.

Destruction of the Temple (Mk. 13:1-2)

Jesus and his disciples visited what was known as the second temple. Solomon built the first temple, which was destroyed at the time of the Babylonian Captivity, six centuries before. When the Jews returned from Babylon, they rebuilt a small temple in 520 B.C. Then Herod the Great decided to restore the temple to the magnificence it deserved.

Herod could have flattened the top of Mount Zion, but he decided instead to build enormous walls around the peak. These walls supported what was basically the stone platform of the thirty-acre temple area. The vertical piers were built with stones forty feet long, eighteen feet wide and twelve feet high. The sheer immensity of the stone work would impress an architect and engineer in any age of history, just as much as in Christ's time. Gold plate adorned the outer walls of the temple building itself, reflecting the sunlight with extraordinary brilliance.

It is easy to see why the disciples expressed such awe at the temple's magnificence and the power of the stonework. Jesus used the moment to teach them that this splendid building would be destroyed at some indeterminate date. In the year 70, Titus conquered Jerusalem and Roman soldiers burned the temple. The support walls still exist, but nothing is left of the temple.

Signs of the End (Mk. 13:3-13)

Christ's words sobered and shocked Peter and Andrew, James and John, the first of the apostles to be called. They sat down on the Mount of Olives and gazed at the magnificence of the temple and the splendor of the Holy City over which the shadow of future disaster hung. They asked Jesus when this would happen and what signs would alert them to its occurrence.

Jesus did not name a date, but he did give three signs that would forecast this catastrophe. His three signs included false doctrine, public chaos, and persecution. Christian tradition has seen in his words a description of the prelude to the end of the world itself.

Subversion of Christian doctrine will be the first sign. This theme is found in verses 3-6 and 21-23. Jesus spoke of the arrival of false prophets and messiahs. Teachers, claiming to represent Christ, will turn the Gospel inside out and persuade the listeners this is authentic revelation. Jesus does not spell out the details of such teachings but we can make some educated guesses.

False teachers may say that love is everything, so one need not worry about sin, redemption, and forgiveness. They might declare that Jesus was the greatest man who ever lived, but he was not a savior, since there is no sin to be saved from. They will probably create a Christian doctrine to suit the fashion of the hour.

Possibly, they will remove the moral demands of religion. Very likely, they will drain the supernatural mystery from religion, reducing everything to what is observable. Hence, they would argue that there is no resurrection of Christ or ourselves, no redemptive act in the cross or Eucharist, no Real Presence of Jesus in the Eucharist, no future life, no divinity of Christ, no grace in the sacraments. Like the false prophets of the Bible, they will say there is peace when there is no peace.

Social and natural chaos constitute the second sign of the end. There will be wars on a global scale. People will rise up against one another. Intensifying the suffering will be natural calamities such as earthquakes. This is the beginning of the suffering. These birthpangs signal both the beginning of the Christian Church as well as the beginning of the final triumph of Christ when the ultimate appearance of the kingdom of God will follow the end of the world itself.

Persecution of the true believers will mark the third sign of the end. The first Christians will suffer at the hands of hostile powers. The same will be true of the last Christians on earth at the end of time. Accused, beaten, intimidated, and martyred, Christians will be asked even to give their lives for the cause of the kingdom, both at the beginning of the preaching of the Gospel and at the end when the Gospel has been brought to every nation on earth.

Families will be torn apart when brother turns against brother, father against child, and children against parents. Christians will be hated because of their commitment to Jesus. Jesus is blunt and unsparing about what he saw in the future for his followers. Jesus was not a lofty oracle talking about the troubles of others. Whatever his followers would suffer, he will first suffer in as terrible a manner, if not more so.

Jesus appreciated the fear and anxiety this would produce. He knew that pain scares everyone. He understood that people have a natural hope they can defend themselves brilliantly, but worry that it will not be possible. He reminded them that the whole response must be one of faith. When standing before the judge, they must not worry too much about how clever they would like to be. The Holy Spirit will give them words and courage to face that hour. Jesus counseled faith-filled endurance and perseverance as the price to be paid for being saved.

O Jerusalem! O Jerusalem! (Mk. 13:14-20)

One must not think Jesus spoke these terrible words with no passion, no dreadful feeling, no regret at such suffering. He is not a detached reporter rattling off the body counts, prisoner lists, battle statistics, and other chronicles of human distress with no emotion or sorrow. Jesus loved people and was as filled with grief about the doom of Jerusalem as anyone else. He felt the same admiration, awe, and attachment to the Holy City as the most devout of pilgrims. So moved was he about the destiny of Jerusalem that he wept over it. It is in this light that his words about Jerusalem's destruction should be read.

When will it happen? What sign will herald it? Jesus taught that the appearance of the desolating sacrilege or abomination of desolation in the temple will tell the tale. He took this image from Daniel 9:27. The image referred to the desecrating of the temple by the pagan conqueror Antiochus. He set up whorehouses in the temple courts and erected a statue of Zeus on the most sacred altar of holocausts and ordered Jews to worship it. This blasphemous act so enraged the Jews that they mounted a successful rebellion under the leadership of Judas Maccabeus.

Jesus taught that a similar desecration would happen again. This time the abomination would be embodied in the form of a Roman general, Titus, who cruelly besieged Jerusalem, slaughtered countless numbers of people, and blitzed the temple building to ashes. So terrible would be the menace to Jerusalem that it would amount to a holocaust of the Jews. Jesus grimly advised that people should flee immediately and leave everything behind. He grieved for the pregnant mother and the woman who would be nursing her child. It would be a greater tragedy than any other remembered.

The Second Coming (Mk. 13:21-27)

Now Jesus turned his attention again to the end of the world, symbolized by the end of the era in which he and his disciples found themselves. We have already seen the three signs of the end that Jesus predicted: the subversion of doctrine, the destructive wars, and the persecution of believers. Jesus added now the apocalyptic imagery of falling stars, blackened moon, and a dead sun.

When all this has happened, the world will have come to an end. Then the Second Coming will take place. Jesus will come again in glory to judge the living and the dead. The way Jesus puts it is in language taken from Daniel 7:13. That prophet describes the arrival of one like a son of man in the skies. He is moving toward God the Father who is pictured as if he were an old patriarch, hence called the "ancient of days." This venerable figure gives the Son of Man dominion and glory and kingdom. All peoples, nations, and languages are expected to serve him.

Jesus, however, sees the Son of Man coming to earth, not just parading across the skies. Angels will gather the elect from the four winds. The traditional interpretation of this text is that Jesus is the real Son of Man come to complete the work of salvation and gather the saints into his kingdom forever.

Take Heed! Watch and Pray! (Mk. 13:28-36)

Jesus refused to give a timetable for these momentous events. But he was insistent that they would occur. The best preparation is to live each day in a fully Christian manner, vigilant, prayerful, and loving. This behavior will rescue his followers from the pitfall of denial and provide them with the readiness they need.

It is difficult to tell from the surviving records how prepared the first Christians were for the devastation that demolished Jerusalem and the temple. Clearly, many of them afterward believed the end of the world and the Second Coming would happen relatively soon. Only as time passed did the communities realize the end of the world did not seem to be so imminent.

Interest in the end of the world and the Second Coming has waxed and waned depending on the circumstances of history. The arrival of the first millennium — the end of the first thousand years of Christian history — occasioned a lively attention to this mystery. The fifty years of the Black Death in the second half of the fourteenth century caused a large part of Christendom to think the end of the world was at hand. That is why so many depictions of the Last Judgement appear at that time.

The Swedish film, "The Seventh Seal" hauntingly captures the "Second Coming" fever that dominated their religious consciousness in those days. The survival into our own century of the hymn "Dies Irae" (Day of Wrath) as a funeral hymn recalls the somber shadow that the medieval view of the end of the world had on their awareness.

It is very likely that the approach of the year 2000 will quicken again a millennerian fever and raise a lot of discussion about the end of time. Whatever happens, Christ's advice is still the best. Take heed. Watch. Pray. We will all die just as we have lived. So the best prescription is to live in faith, hope, love, trust, and surrender to God. Love conquers all, even death itself. Failure to live the Christian lifestyle means that the end will be terrifying and will cause despair. Success means that the end is a birth and a beginning when Jesus will gather us together forever with the saints.

Reflection

1. What do I think of those religious sects that predict the exact date of the end of the world and gather on a mountaintop to greet it?
2. What are some examples of gloom and doom (apocalyptic) language in our own culture?

3. The apostles dreaded the thought of the destruction of the temple How would I feel about my Catholicism if St. Peter's in Rome were destroyed and not a stone left upon a stone?
4. Why didn't Christ give a timetable for the end of the temple, Jerusalem, and the end of our world?
5. How would I react if a pope issued an encyclical that announced the end of the world would take place in exactly ten years from the date of the encyclical's publication?
6. Since there are almost always perversions of doctrine, big wars and persecution of Christians somewhere, how could I tell whether this grouping of signs is the one that truly signals the end?
7. How might I have felt if I lived during the time of the Black Death in the second half of the fourteenth century?
8. What is the best way to prepare for the Second Coming?
9. How do I personally visualize the Second Coming?
10. What is the purpose of the Last Judgement?

Prayer

Lord Jesus, judge of the living and the dead, you have asked me always to listen, watch, and pray so that I am always ready for my death as well as for the end of the world. Prompt my awareness of this each day, so that my commitment to a Christian lifestyle will prepare me to face this with faith, trust, and surrender.

14 From the Table to the Cross

A Woman Anoints Christ (Mk. 14:1-11)

The most solemn religious festival, the Passover, was about to begin. Christ's enemies planned to arrest and kill him. Jesus meanwhile attended a dinner in the home of Simon the leper at Bethany. Like the other dinner guests, Jesus reclined on a low couch. Customarily, someone would honor a guest by sprinkling the person with a few drops of perfume.

A woman came up to Jesus and broke the neck of a flask of perfume (the nard) that had been imported from India. Instead of spraying a few drops on him, she anointed him with the contents of the entire bottle, the cost of which was equal to a year's wages. This was an anointing fit for a king. It was also the kind of anointing used for a rich person during that person's burial rite at the tomb. It was a total gift. Neither the jar nor the perfume would be used again.

Several expressed dismay at the extravagance of the woman. They said it would have been more useful to have sold the nard and given the money to the poor. Jesus replied that they have a chance to help the poor every day, but the time is short and they have little opportunity left to do anything for him. He told them that she has anointed his body for burial, even before he has died. He declared that her story would be known all over the world wherever the Gospel is preached.

Mark's text then contrasts the love of the woman with the treachery of Judas. The woman demonstrated how to love Jesus absolutely and give all. Judas never learned how to love Jesus. Instead, he exploited the friendship offered him and betrayed it.

The Christian Passover is the Lord's Supper (Mk. 14:12-31)

Passover remembered and celebrated two Israelite liberations, one from the avenging angel of the tenth plague and the other from slavery in Egypt. The two major rituals for Passover were adapted from nature festivals. In their shepherd society, the birth of new lambs was an occasion of joy. A lamb was offered to God in thanksgiving. Similarly, in their barley harvest, a way was found to thank God for the new crop. A sheaf of barley was waved before God as a sign of appreciation for the new grain. At home the old yeast (or leaven) was thrown away. New bread from the new grain was baked without use of leaven.

In the Exodus story, the Israelites had marked their doors with the blood of a lamb. This protected them from the avenging angel. They baked unleavened bread which could be done quickly, since the leavening process was skipped. They stood while eating their departure meal because they had to hurry out of Egypt.

In Jesus' time, a Passover lamb was purchased and taken to the temple for sacrifice. One of the apostles would have then killed the lamb and poured the blood into a container. A priest took the blood and poured it on an altar. Blood signified life. Hence this was the offering of the gift of life to God, the lamb substituting for that of the human giver. The fat and insides of the lamb were removed and burnt on the altar. The rising, sweet smoke rose to God as another form of a pleasing gift. The body of the lamb was then brought home, where it was roasted on a spit over an open fire of pomegranate wood.

Jesus had despatched two disciples to make all these arrangements, just as he had planned the Palm Sunday entry. They acquired an upper room for the celebration. While most homes were one-story dwellings, a fair number had a single room built on the roof and accessible from an outdoor stairway. Many families used the room as a rooftop attic for storage. Some reserved the room as a "classroom" where rabbis taught their disciples. Jesus arranged for just such a room for his Last Supper.

Jesus and his disciples reclined on couches around a table built low to the ground. The consecrated lamb was the centerpiece on the table and prompted them to think of the divine love that had liberated their ancestors from slavery. It would also become in Christian memory a vivid symbol of Christ's sacrifice as lamb of God for the salvation of the world from the slavery of sin.

The fellowship of apostles would also have seen on the table three fresh baked loaves of unleavened bread, a bowl of salt water in memory of the tears that were shed in the flight from Egypt and dishes of horseradish and endive to recall the bitterness of dehumanizing slavery. Next they would have gazed at plates filled with sticks of cinnamon bordering a red colored paste made from apples, dates, and nuts which symbolized the straw and clay from which they made bricks in the forced labor pits in Egypt. Four cups of wine stood before each member of the feast.

In biblical times, a new day began at sundown, hence — in our terms — Friday began on Thursday evening. And that is when the Passover meal began. Normally this was a cheerful meal, even if its ritual stages were marked with solemn liturgical moments. However, Jesus introduced the meal with a troubling announcement that one of his apostles would betray him. It was a shocking beginning to the feast and it caused the fellowship of trusted friends to be full of sorrow.

None of them could imagine this was possible. Judas had been so successful in concealing his disenchantment with Christ that no apostle guessed it. Jesus alone could tell that Judas was not truly committed to him. A skilled judge of people, Jesus could read the insincerity of Judas in his eyes, his small betrayals of daily fraternity, his preoccupation with money, his habit of secrecy, his lack of enthusiasm for a peace-loving Messiah.

Jesus could feel tension between himself and Judas. His friend looked withdrawn and his face showed disapproval of what he thought was a Palm Sunday fiasco. What should have been a perfect occasion for messianic muscle flexing became a tame peace march. It infuriated Judas and led him to the conspirator's meeting with the religious leaders.

Jesus knew this was not an open and above-board man. To be let down and betrayed by someone you trust is always a bitter and disappointing discovery. Most people react with rage and fury, lashing out at the traitor. Jesus had saved his prophetic rage for religious leaders who oppressed simple people.

But Jesus had spent time offering Judas his love, concern, affection, and revelatory truth, just as he had to all the apostles. Jesus had placed his confidence in Judas, had never lied to him or hid from him exactly where he stood. Jesus still loved Judas and hoped that his warning signal would deter him from the self-destructive path that lay ahead.

Clearly, Jesus could have forced Judas out into the open, exposed his treachery, and thrown him to the tender mercies of the other apostles whose anger would have taught Judas a lesson he would never forget. Jesus had no intention of piling apostolic vengeance on top of apostolic betrayal. He did not want the see the Upper Room become a scene of passionate anger, recrimination, and brawling. He had come to create a community of love and forgiveness. He trusted in the power of love and believed that the response to this love must be free and not forced.

Each apostle asked Jesus, "Is it I, Lord?" Jesus responded by saying that whoever dipped bread into the same dish with him was the one. Since several might have done this, the problem was not solved. The traitor was protected by Jesus with an ambiguous statement. This was another form of love's last appeal to Judas to repent and change his behavior.

Thus the experience of betrayal prefaced the institution of the Sacrament of Love. Jesus did not let Judas' refusal of his love to stand in the way of his intention to bequeath to the world a feast of love and forgiveness. The betrayal only added a sense of urgency to make sure that such an inheritance of love be left to the apostles.

This Is My Body and Blood . . . This is I! (Mk. 14:22-25)

Before him were the newly baked loaves of unleavened bread. Jesus took the bread and blessed it. His blessing words were similar to those used in our Masses today. "Blessed are you, O Lord God of all creation. You have given us this bread to eat, fruit of the earth and the work of human hands." In any other Passover meal, he would then have broken the bread and passed it around with words about the sufferings of their forefathers in Egypt. There would be an invitation to a hungry person to come and join them. Frequently, a poor stranger would be brought into the feast at that time.

That night, Jesus changed the rules and departed from the ritual that everyone present knew by heart from earliest childhood. He broke the bread saying, "Take. This is my body." Not only did he introduce new words into the ceremony, but a word-action, mysterious and momentous for the participants. It was a word-action because the words he spoke transformed the bread and invited his apostles to commune with him. He also invited them to an action, namely, to participate in and identify with his saving deeds. Then he distributed the bread become his Body. The ritual continued with the narration of the story of the salvation from Egypt. At its conclusion, Jesus recited a meal prayer and the supper of the lamb began.

At the end of the meal, the remainder of the unleavened bread (now changed by Jesus into his body) was eaten. There were four cups of wine at each place setting. The first one was drunk at the beginning of the meal and the second one during the supper of the lamb. It was at the close of this part of the meal that Jesus took the third cup of wine and said words similar to these: "Blessed are you, Lord God of all creation, you have given us this wine to drink, fruit of the vine and the work of human hands."

Normally, they would have drunk the wine and sung the praise psalms 115-118. Again Jesus changed the ritual by adding a new word-action before the singing of the psalms. After the blessing he added, "This is my blood of the covenant." Called to pour out their lives as well in unity with him, they drank the third cup of Passover wine in a totally new and unique manner. The fourth cup of wine, like a toast, concluded the meal.

The depth of his words plus his change of what was considered the strictest of all religious patterns could only elicit silence as each apostle wrestled with this profound experience. New Testament history showed that the breaking of the bread — or Christian Passover was celebrated immediately after Pentecost. Explanations of the Lord's command about the bread and wine as his body and blood took time to develop. This deepest of Christian mysteries was first absorbed in silence and faith. Only the contemplative uses of time would yield the words to describe the meaning of what happened on that holy night.

At a meal where they ate a sacrificial lamb that taught them about divine redemption, Jesus spoke about his body that would be eaten and his blood that would be poured out. He provided the lead concepts that would show the connection with his redemptive death on Good Friday. In a setting where love, forgiveness, and fellowship were experiences as prominent as the theme of sacrifice, Jesus taught that the Breaking of the Bread and the Drinking of the Cup were essentially bound with Christian love and community. Thus the Last Supper was inexorably tied to the building of Christian community and the redemptive sacrifice of Jesus. It was both a fellowship and sacrificial event.

After completing the singing of the thanksgiving psalms, the group went to the Mount of Olives. Jesus told them that they would abandon him. Enemies would strike the shepherd and the sheep would be scattered. Jesus understood that their purely human strength would not see them through the tragedy just ahead. They still did not have the spiritual depth that was needed. Only when the Holy Spirit took hold of them would they become the pillars of the church that was their destiny.

He did not leave them with that gloomy assessment. He would rise from the dead and meet them in Galilee where the ministry of salvation began so promisingly a few years before. Peter protested that he would never desert Jesus, even if all the others weakened. Jesus told him that his defection would be more dramatic than the others. He would deny him three times before the cock crowed at sunrise. Ever sure of himself, Peter loudly reaffirmed his loyalty even if it meant death. The others said the same.

So the Last Supper began with a story of an apostolic betrayal and concluded with a prediction of apostolic denial and abandonment. The Sacrament of Love stood like a shining jewel in the shadows of human failure and sinfulness.

This Cup I Pray Please Take Away (Mk. 14:32-52)

Jesus walked to the cross with his sense of divine purpose. He also journeyed there with all the feelings of dread that any human being would have. He went to Gethsemane with the same three disciples who had witnessed the glory of his Transfiguration. Now he wanted them to share with him the struggle he must go through to fully accept the Father's will. He was not ashamed to express his need for their support when the greatest sorrow afflicted him.

All his human drives recoiled from the suffering and death that awaited him. It would take the full power of his spiritual resources to fight these survival instincts and put his body and whole self at the service of love's greatest demands. Like anybody at death's door he felt depression and fear. He wanted Peter, James and John to know that and to pray with him in this struggle. "He began to be greatly depressed and sorrowful" (verse 33). He had shared his inmost feelings with them.

He threw himself on the ground and begged his Father to take away the cup of suffering. But at the same time, he said that only the Father's will should be done, not his own. He arose and looked for his support group. They slept. He looked at the sleeping Peter, who had professed so much loyalty barely an hour ago. He woke Peter up and asked if he could not be with him for at least one hour when he needed a good friend the most.

He admonished Peter, whose eyes were heavy with sleep after their big meal, to watch and pray that he might not enter into temptation. Vigilance and prayer are the best safeguards against temptation. Jesus let Peter know that he understood how positive were his intentions. Peter's spirit was willing, but the flesh was weak. Three times Jesus prayed for deliverance from the pain. Three times he found his apostles asleep. He had surrendered to his Father's will. He woke the sleeping apostles and asked them to stand with him. His betrayal was at hand.

Judas Gives Jesus a Traitor's Kiss (Mk. 14: 43-51)

While Christ's dearest friends slept, his traitorous apostle, Judas, was wide awake. This will always be a problem in Christian history. The guardians of the people will slumber when they should be alert in calling people to virtue and training them in the acquisition of Gospel values. Those who wish to destroy the Christian dream and ideals will be active and energetic in their efforts to subvert and undermine the Gospel.

Judas arrived with a crowd carrying swords and clubs. He told them that the man he hugged and kissed was the one to be arrested. With no shame, he walked right up to Jesus, addressed him as "Master" and kissed him. Jesus offered no resistance. He did not try to escape. He did not call for defenders. He had given Judas every opportunity to repent and the weak apostle let his human calculations determine his behavior. Judas was not open to love. He never let Jesus really love him. Judas used Christ's trusting nature as a weapon to betray him.

One of the bystanders drew a sword and cut off the ear of a slave. John 18:10 says it was Peter who did this to a man named Malchus. Luke 22:50-51 reports that Jesus healed the servant's ear. Jesus asked the aggressors why they came with swords and clubs as though to capture a robber. Why did they not seize him when he was openly preaching in the temple? In other words that same group had been at the temple. They did in darkness what they failed to do in the light.

Just as Jesus predicted, all his apostles deserted him. One young man followed him, but when the captors tried to seize him, he ran away naked leaving his robe in their clutching hands. Many have tried to guess who this was, some believing it was Mark, the writer of this Gospel.

Night Court (Mk. 14:53-63)

They brought Jesus to a hastily assembled meeting of the religious court. A night court was an exception to their usual procedure. The council sought testimony that would lead to Christ's death. They were having trouble doing this because the perjuring witnesses they enlisted contradicted each other's accusations. At least two witnesses had to agree on the existence of a crime.

The witnesses accused him of intending to destroy the temple and rebuild a new one "not made with hands." It sounds like they took Christ's prediction of the destruction of the temple, which they may have heard about from Judas and combined it with his "violent" act of cleansing the temple and formed that into an accusation that he literally would gather a destructive force with that intention. Whatever they actually said, they presented sufficiently vague and confusing accounts, so that the judge could not indict Jesus for a crime.

The high priest asked Jesus if he had any response to these accusations. Jesus remained silent. This majestic silence of the passion recalls Isaiah's predictions of a Holy Martyr who would go to his death like a lamb, uncomplaining, and without defense.

Then the high priest asked Jesus if he was the Messiah. This time Jesus spoke and said that he was the Messiah. He went further and identified himself with the Son of Man described in Daniel 7:13. The high priest used this opportunity to declare that Jesus had blasphemed. He symbolized his accusation by theatrically tearing his robe.

Strictly speaking this was not blasphemy which would be reviling the holy name of God. Admitting he was the Messiah was not a blasphemy. What probably seemed to be blasphemy in this situation was Christ's claim he would sit at God's right hand and judge the nations. Whatever their reason, the court agreed that Jesus had committed a blasphemy and condemned him as deserving of death. Some began to spit on him, put a hood on his head and asked him to tell them who struck him. The guards took him over and beat him.

The only purpose Jesus ever had in life was to offer people the chance for love, justice, and mercy by means of his redemptive action. It is now clear that he would achieve this redemption by first suffering hatred, injustice, cruel mockery, and beating.

I Do Not Know Jesus (Mk. 14: 66-72)

Peter followed Jesus to the scene of the trial and warmed himself by the fire outside the courtroom. Three times people said to Peter they recognized him as a follower of Jesus. Each time, Peter vigorously denied he even knew Jesus. The cock crowed and Peter remembered that Jesus had predicted this would happen. He broke down and wept.

Reflection

1. The anointing at Bethany symbolized the full commitment of love

that was shown to Jesus by the woman. In what ways can I develop this kind of love for Christ?

2. What nature festivals were incorporated into the feast of the Passover? How were they linked to the feast?
3. What two liberations did the Jews celebrate in their Passover celebration?
4. What unhappy events introduce and close the Last Supper story? What light do these events cast on the meaning of the Last Supper?
5. What is an Upper Room? What were the various uses for such a room?
6. When Jesus took the newly baked unleavened bread, what did he do that was new and unusual?
7. Christ's words of institution of the Eucharist at the Last Supper were "action-words." What does this mean?
8. How is the Passover Meal a Fellowship Meal?
9. What is there about the Passover Meal that gave it a character of sacrifice?
10. How did Jesus make the Eucharist stand for both Fellowship and Sacrifice at the Last Supper?
11. If I were at the Last Supper and heard Jesus new "action-words" how would I react? What would I think? Would I think differently than an apostle did?
12. If I were at Gethsemane that evening with the apostles, what might I have done?
13. How does a person get to be like Judas?
14. Why couldn't Peter listen to Jesus and realize he might deny him?

Prayer

Christ of the Passion, your hour has come. You have persevered in your intention to save the world from sin and have accepted the Father's will to forge ahead. I praise you and love you for your own great act of love. I pray that I may identify myself with you and offer you my own troubles and trials that, with your power, they may contribute to the spread of love, healing, and forgiveness in the world.

15 Hail Blessed Wood that Bore Our Savior

He Suffered Under Pontius Pilate (Mk. 15:1-20)

It is now Good Friday morning.

The captors brought Jesus to the Fortress Antonia, the residence of the Roman governor, Pontius Pilate. The governor used this house during the Passover pilgrimage to supervise public order and control rebellious behavior. Otherwise, he ruled from his palace at Caesarea Maritima. Only he could judge whether Jesus deserved the death penalty, and only he could give the order for Christ's execution.

Pilate asked Jesus if he is king of the Jews. Christ's captors had condemned him for blasphemy, but this religious accusation would mean nothing to a pagan ruler. Pilate would only react to the breaking of Roman law. Hence the accusers brought a charge that would imply that Jesus had organized a political rebellion.

The charge would seem plausible to Pilate. Jesus had permitted himself to be hailed as a messianic king on Palm Sunday, so long as that was understood in a spiritual and peaceful sense. But the sight of an enthusiastic crowd hailing a leader in a triumphant march into a city where rebellious unrest was common could easily lead the governor to conclude that this was a dangerous man. Secondly, his cleansing of the temple, albeit for commendable religious reasons, could reinforce the feeling that this man had hostile political intentions.

Christ's reply to Pilate was noncommittal. Jesus affirmed he was King of the Jews in such a way that the political meaning of the phrase was rejected. Then the chief priests accused him of many things, none of which are specified in Mark. Jesus remained silent. The passion narratives record three silences of Jesus, one before the Sanhedrin (Mk. 14:61); one before Pilate (Mk. 15:5); and one before Herod (Lk. 23:9). John's Gospel reports that Jesus did say other things during his trial. These silences of the Passion identify Jesus with the Suffering Servant of Isaiah, chapter 53.

From other sources we know that Pilate was a cruel and obstinate man. In the gospel accounts he comes across as indecisive and concerned with justice in the case of Jesus Christ. In this unique encounter, Pilate faced a man who reached him in a manner he had never experienced before. What should have been an open and shut case of ridding himself of a local troublemaker, became a test of conscience for him, a test that he would fail unfortunately. The witnessing power of Jesus affected the governor.

Jesus was never indifferent to any human being. He had come to save Pilate just as much as Mary Magdalene. The few spare words of Mark reveal little about how Jesus impacted Pilate. Without a doubt, the power of Christ's personal presence touched him. Pilate watched Christ's silence in the face of a babble of accusations. Mark catches the mystery of Pilate's conscience with a minimalist description. "Pilate wondered" (verse 5).

This seems to be the best explanation for the unusual step Pilate took in announcing a Passover amnesty. Extra-biblical sources have no record of such amnesties as part of public policy in the Roman province of Judea. Pilate's encounter with Jesus motivated him to select an ad-hoc exception to what would have been a routine summary judgement on a suspected guerilla leader.

Pilate selected a terrorist, named Barabbas, as an alternative prisoner for amnesty. Barabbas was a revolutionary and a murderer, just the kind of man the Roman's feared most. In front of the Fortress Antonia was a courtyard about a half an acre in size. It was called the Lithostrotos, or place of paved, polished stones. At best, only a few hundred people could fit there. This is different from the impression given by artists and movie versions of throngs of thousands crowding before Pilate. Recall that this was early morning. Not too many people would even know of the trial. Nor could many fit in the place set for the choice of prisoners. In any case it makes little difference whether the crowd was big or small. The tragic outcome was the same.

Pilate could reasonably have assumed the people would have picked Jesus. Had they not hailed him with love the previous Sunday? The chief priests, however, influenced the crowd to pick Barrabas. Pilate asked them what he should do with Jesus. They yelled out for his crucifixion. Pilate found himself trying to protect Jesus. He asked them what evil had this man done. The crucifixion chant was all he could hear. He capitulated to the mob.

He condemned Jesus to the cross, not because of proven criminal charges, but due to the pressure of a mob. He was a weak man, who normally masked his attitude by an arbitrary use of cruelty and power. His one attack of conscience in his encounter with Christ revealed his weakness and lack of moral strength. When the chips were down he simply reverted to the cowardice of tyrants. Kill a troublemaker and preserve crowd control.

Events now moved swiftly. Pilate turned Jesus over to the soldiers and gave the order for crucifixion. The Romans recruited soldiers from Palestine and Syria. It was about nine o'clock in the morning and the crucifixion was set for noon. Soldiers normally prepared a prisoner for crucifixion by weakening him as much as possible so that his stay on the cross would be lessened. The crucified prisoners usually died from suffocation when they were no longer able to lift themselves up to breathe. Despite that, they often lived as much as a week and are reported to have conversations with friends and relatives during the death watch.

Because this was Passover, death had to be guaranteed by sundown, since an exposed, dying body would profane the feast. All the gospels report the scourging, which was part of the process of weakening the victim. The soldiers mocked Jesus and crowned him with thorns. It is not clear which thorns they used. Thorn bushes lined the Mount of Olives. Some have wondered if the thorns from the date palms were used. If that be so, then the palms of glory on Sunday would be replaced with the thorns of the date palms on Friday.

To the soldiers this was nothing more than a dreary and dirty business. They amused themselves by taunting the prisoner. They released their own aggressions and frustrations by taking them out on Jesus. They dressed him up in a purple cloak and put the crown of thorns on his head. They beat him, laughed at him, knelt before him, and made fun of him. The center and source of all love and affection in the universe was beaten, spit on, ridiculed, and cursed. It was a terrible moment in the history of our relationship with Christ.

And They Nailed Him To a Cross (Mk. 15:21-41)

Jesus carried the horizontal cross beam on his way to Calvary. At the site of execution was a vertical post into which the cross beam was inserted. At some point in the march to Golgotha (the word means skull hill), Jesus must have looked too exhausted to carry the cross any further. The soldiers enlisted an onlooker, Simon, a Jew from Cyrene in Africa, to carry the cross for him the rest of the way. Simon was most likely in the city as a pilgrim for the Passover. Mark mentions that Simon was the father of Alexander and Rufus. Paul mentions Rufus in Romans 16:13. Apparently, he had moved to Rome with his mother and they were part of the new Christian community. Paul expresses so deep an affection for the mother of Rufus that he speaks of her as his own mother as well.

They brought Jesus to Calvary, also called Golgotha, or the place of the skull. Some believe that this execution mound was once used as a place for beheading, hence the name "skull hill." A legend states that Adam's skull was imbedded in the earth. This lead to the popular piety that the blood of the second Adam flowed down upon the first Adam. Regardless of the legendary wording, the truth of the story is that Christ redeemed Adam and all human beings before and after the act of salvation at skull hill.

Then they crucified him, nailing his wrists to the cross bar and his feet to the vertical post. Had they placed the nails in the palms of his hands, the weight of his body would have torn through the finger areas. The wrist bones kept the nails in place. A small wooden bar midway down the post gave the crucified a place to "sit." And a wooden pedestal for the feet gave further leverage to the crucified's body. However, the pull of gravity on the body as the hours and days wore on made it increasingly difficult for the crucified to pull himself up to breathe properly. Eventually, he would die of asphyxiation.

A detail of four soldiers guarded the cross. Among themselves, they divided Christ's clothing, which included a turban, a tunic, a belt, and sandals. They gambled for the fifth article of clothing, his seamless robe. The twenty-second psalm, verse 18, which is a prayer of anguish and hope from the lips of an ancient Jewish martyr, depicts a similar scene. Probably, the guards customarily did this at execution sites. That is, of course, small comfort for the prisoner and even more heartbreaking for the family members who would want these personal mementoes for themselves. Given the strong possibility that the Blessed Mother wove her son's seamless robe, the impact on her would be doubly poignant.

The soldiers always brought with them a jug of wine mingled with myhrr. The narcotic mixture was meant to dull the pain of the crucified. Jesus refused this wine presentation. In John's account of the passion, a second wine presentation occurs. This time Jesus accepts the wine in conjunction with his words of spiritual outreach, "I thirst."

Above Christ's head the soldiers posted a sign bearing the name of his crime, "King of the Jews," in Hebrew, Greek, and Latin. Pilate ordered the sign to say just those words, because that is what the priests used as an accusation. The sign's main purpose was to caution potential political rebels against activity that could only lead to this devastating end. Ironically, a Roman governor posted a proclamation of Christ's messianic identity in the three main languages of the Mediterranean world. The governor had not crucified a rebel. Pilate had killed a Savior.

During his ministry Jesus had always felt at home with sinners. He loved to say that he had not come to save the saved, but to bring love to sinners. He reminded everyone that it was the sick that needed a doctor, not the healthy ones. He, who sought out the company of sinners, had two sinners for companionship at Calvary. Two convicted thieves flanked his cross, being crucified themselves. He was completing the act of salvation in the sight of two men who were clearly in need of love, mercy, and justice.

Jesus had always witnessed compassion and sensitivity to those in pain. He talked about the beauty of healing love and practiced a healing ministry with kind words, affectionate touches and a positive spirit. Evil people, however, did not listen to him. They rejected his vision and succeeded in bringing him to this painful end. In the hour of their triumph they lacked graciousness. They had no sense of shame about what they were doing.

We must remember these were ostensibly religious people, many of them religious leaders. A major goal of religion has always been moral purity and compassionate behavior. Yet here the priests, scribes, and their fellow "parishioners" screamed at Jesus. They yelled at him to come down from the cross, he who would tear down the temple and rebuild it.

They mockingly called him King of the Jews and dared him to save himself. They perverted Christ's use of salvation language. He had spoken of salvation as a loving deliverance of people from all that oppressed them, above all from sin. They reduced salvation to an act of self interest. "Save yourself!" They asked the "man for others" to indulge his ego needs. The priests were the guardians of the Torah, a term that means light. They were the keepers of the divine flame, meant to guide people to love and moral goodness. Their actions at Calvary proved them to be blind guides who walked in darkness and lacked even the human decency to let a man die in peace and let his family have some moments of calm to commune with their dearly beloved Jesus.

Death, Where Is Thy Sting? (Mk. 15:33-41)

Darkness descended on Calvary, as if nature itself mourned the imminent death of Jesus. Close to three o'clock, Jesus cried out with a loud voice, "My God, my God, why have you forsaken me?" (verse 34). The words come from the opening of Psalm 22, which is the prayer of a holy martyr. Many believe that Jesus proceeded to pray the entire psalm. In any case he used words that express the sense of abandonment a dying person will feel. The words tell of losing a sense of God's presence. Not only have the apostles (save John) abandoned Jesus, even the heavenly Father seems to have done the same.

In any relationship, the lover expects the beloved to be present, especially in a time of acute stress and need. A suffering lover needs the support of the beloved's consoling warmth and presence. Jesus expected as much from his Father. In fact the Father did not withdraw his loving presence and support for Jesus. It was the physical pain, the emotional distress and the desolation caused by the spiritual blindness of his persecutors that temporarily blocked out the experience of his Father's consoling presence.

The Father continued to offer his love. The Son still received it, filtered through a screen of pain that neutralized a feeling of presence. As evidence that Jesus still felt loved, his words that followed this abandonment in the other gospels demonstrate his trust, affection and surrender to his Father. Even Psalm 22 itself concludes with words of faithful trust.

Taken together, the four gospels narrate seven last words or utterances from Jesus. Mark reports only this abandonment text. In his account, Jesus lets out a brutal shout (like a primal scream) from the cross and dies. Mark does not sentimentalize the death of Jesus. Unlike Luke, he does not tell of Christ's devout night prayer, commending himself to his Father. Unlike John, he does not narrate the liturgical ending of consummation of a sacrifice. Mark gives us the death rattle pure and simple with nothing to soften it. Jesus died — terribly, painfully, truly.

As the echo of Christ's last sound faded, the veil of the temple was torn from top to bottom. This veil was a curtain that separated the holiest part of the temple building from the rest of the space. What did this prodigy signify? Possibly, it symbolized God the Father tearing his "robe" in sorrow and mourning over the death of his Son. Another suggested symbolism is that it was a way of teaching that Christ's death revealed God's saving presence to the world. This interpretation flows from the belief that God's presence was hidden behind the veil at the temple. Remove the curtain and God is revealed for all who have faith to see him.

This second symbolism seems to fit the story of the faith testimony of the centurion who is moved to affirm — after the death of Jesus — that Christ is truly the Son of God. At the very moment of its occurrence, Christ's death becomes a revelation of who he is and what he has done. Death has removed the veil that, for some, hid his messiahship and divinity. The experience evokes faith.

The mother of Jesus, Mary Magdalen, and two other women witnessed all these events. Their love kept them close to Jesus. They had always looked after his needs. They remained his faithful support group to the end.

The Funeral (Mk. 15:42-47)

Jesus died three hours before sundown when the sabbath would begin. No work could be done on the sabbath, so the burial arrangements had to be done swiftly. Seemingly out of nowhere came Joseph of Arimathea, a prosperous Jew and a member of the Sanhedrin. He would have been present at the religious trial of Jesus, both at the night court and the morning session that arranged for Christ's transfer to a trial before Pilate. Joseph would be our source for the details of what happened at the trial.

He was a secret admirer of Jesus, but not committed enough to Christ to convince the Sanhedrin to let him go. The message of the living Jesus attracted him, but it was the dying and the death of Jesus that converted him. Joseph came to the death watch at the Cross and experienced a conversion of his heart.

He immediately went to Pilate and asked permission to bury Jesus in his own tomb. Pilate was amazed that Jesus had died so quickly. Normally, crucifixion victims lasted as much as a week before they died. The centurion confirmed that Jesus was dead. Pilate granted permission for the burial. With the help of his servants, Joseph removed Christ's body from the Cross. Joseph personally wrapped the body of Jesus in a shroud and placed him on the stone of anointing in the tomb. There was no time for an anointing. The little party of mourners that included Christ's mother, Mary Magdalene, and two other women took one last look at Jesus Christ and left the grave room. A heavy circular stone was rolled against the entrance.

Reflection

1. How do Christ's silences in the passion affect me?
2. Why did Jesus affect Pilate differently from other prisoners?
3. What moved the crowd to choose Barabbas over Jesus?
4. What motivated Pilate to give in to the crowd?
5. Why did the soldiers treat Jesus so cruelly?
6. In my meditations on the scourging of Jesus at the pillar, what thoughts come to me?

7. When I gaze on the scene of the crowning of thorns, how is my faith deepened?
8. How do I feel when I contemplate the soldiers gambling for the seamless robe of Jesus?
9. As I hear Jesus speak of his feeling abandoned by God, what events in my life have produced a similar effect?
10. How would I explain the tearing of the veil of the temple?
11. What does my heart tell me when I listen to the centurion's act of faith in Jesus, truly the Son of God?
12. What was there about the dying and death of Jesus that converted the heart of Joseph of Arimathea?

Prayer

Jesus Christ, Crucified God, absolute lover of the world and each human being, I adore you and praise you, for by your holy cross you have redeemed the world. Your dying and death speaks to my heart and moves it to love, faith, and conversion. I praise you. I love you. I worship you. In silence, I rest with you.

16 Like Wheat that Arises Green

On the Third Day, He Rose From the Dead (Mk. 16:1-14)

Lack of time prevented a Friday anointing, so the women came at dawn on Sunday to complete their task. In their hurry to the tomb, they forgot to bring someone to help them roll the heavy stone back from the entrance. They wondered if they would have the strength to do so. Amazed, they found the stone removed. Entering the grave room they found a young man dressed in white (named an angel in other gospel accounts) standing next to the stone of anointing. The body of Jesus was gone.

Pointing to the empty space, he announced to the stunned women that Jesus had risen from the dead. He told them to bring this Good News to the disciples, and especially to Peter (explicitly mentioned by name). Jesus will meet them in Galilee where his whole beautiful ministry began. The young man invited the women to go beyond amazement and astonishment. "Do not be amazed" (verse 6). Just as Jesus always wanted his apostles to get beyond the wonder stage (as in the calming of the storm at sea) and open their hearts to faith, the young man at the tomb urged the same growth on the women.

They would need faith to believe that Jesus was not dead, but alive. They fled from the grave room, overcome by trembling and astonishment, but slowly these feelings gave way to faith. That very day, Jesus honored Mary Magdalene with his first Easter appearance. He had come to save sinners and reserved his first public resurrection appearance for a sinner from whom he had driven seven devils. Mary Magdalene was ready. Her faith had grown from a small seed into a flourishing tree. John's gospel lovingly tells this encounter of Jesus and Magdalene in extensive detail (Jn. 20:11-18). She became the first evangelist of the resurrection as she joyfully ran to the apostles and rang out the Good News. They did not believe her.

Their faith still needed further maturing.

Jesus then appeared to two disciples walking in the countryside. This appearance was probably the same one as that described by Luke in the Emmaus story (Lk. 24:15-35). They also returned to the apostolic group with the great news and found the same disbelief that Magdalene did.

At last Jesus appeared to the eleven apostles and rebuked them for their lack of faith. Jesus gave them an experience of his risen presence and then invited them to faith in its reality. He showed that he still loved them, so much in fact that he overcame death so he could be with them and all people forever. His obvious affection touched them, awoke their belief and drew them to his heart. The very pillars upon which the Christian church would be built, the apostles, were slow to believe and needed a catechesis from the risen Christ himself to move them to faith. That catechesis worked because they experienced Christ's warm love opening them to accept the most profound of mysteries.

Their acceptance of the resurrection was a process of faith growth, not a quick and easy belief with no struggle. Their fundamental difficulty was accepting the truth that Jesus really loved them. When they had finally straightened out their interpersonal relations with Jesus, when they truly believed he loved them and were willing to let him love them, they could accept the resurrection and all the mysteries of salvation.

This meeting with Jesus settled the love question once and for all. Only love could conquer death. When they realized that and awakened to the enormous affection Jesus had for them, they yielded to the most truly amazing relationship one can have. These gospel accounts of the difficulties the apostles had accepting the resurrection should be consoling to each of us as we strive to put all doubts behind us and grow into a free and open and joyful faith in the glorious revelation of Jesus Christ risen from the dead. When we feel and accept Christ's love, all else follows easily.

The Great Commission (Mk. 16: 15-20)

When Jesus had convinced the apostles that he loved them more than they could ever have imagined and obtained their joyful opening to his love, he confirmed the apostles' faith, which now flowed so easily. He commissioned these faith witnesses of the resurrection to preach the Gospel to the whole creation. They are to call people to baptism and salvation.

Above all, they should invite people to experience and enjoy the forgiving and liberating love that they themselves had experienced. Love is always a more convincing argument than logic. It is love that is the key to drawing people to faith in the truth of Christ's teaching. Once the person of Jesus is accepted, then all else flows with ease. Love of Christ leads inevitably to accepting Christ's teachings and truths. Love is the best window onto truth. Some may be able to go through truth to love. Perhaps their intellectual mind-set requires this. But most human beings take the path from love to truth.

The secret of the apostles' immense success in preaching the gospel was that they shared Good News about a terrific person who loves each human being with inexhaustible energy. The apostles did more than preach about Jesus, they shared the personal stories of their own development of a love relationship with Christ. They shared their weaknesses, their betrayals, and their abandonments of their best friend. They told of how Christ reached out to them every time and touched them with the warmth of his heart. He loved them back to a firm and lasting relationship.

When the Bible says they witnessed Christ's resurrection, they were singing a love song. They were praising God for the victory of love in their own lives. Jesus had not only loved them constantly, he helped them to accept his love. He loosened their resistance to a love which alone could make them feel fully alive. He taught them to let go of their anxieties and feel freedom. He instructed them to let go of their hostilities and reach out generously to all people. He enlightened them about the futility of suspicion of others and urged them to appeal rather to the best in other people's natures.

Love became a golden thread that bound them to their listeners and captivated their hearts. That is why they became such astonishing convert makers. They used the most irresistible force ever invented to change people's minds — by changing people's hearts first. This is why Easter time always seems as close to paradise as we get to on earth. This puts the fire and enthusiasm into evangelization.

When Jesus felt absolutely certain they were ready to go on their own, he ascended to heaven and sat down at God's right hand. Saint Luke adds that Jesus would send the Holy Spirit to complete and round out the work of love he had begun on earth.

"Worthy are you, Lord our God, to receive glory and honor and power, forever and ever. Amen" (Rv. 4:11, 13).

Reflection

1. Why did the young man at the tomb tell the women not to be amazed?
2. What is there in the act of wonder and amazement that feels like faith?
3. What can I personally learn from the apostles' inability to believe in the resurrection when they first heard of it?
4. Our faith journey could follow one of two paths, one in which love leads to truth and one in which truth leads to love. Which path suits me and why?
5. Why is it fair to say that the risen Jesus resorted to love and affection to open the apostles to his resurrection?
6. What is the Great Commission?
7. How do I tend to share my faith?
8. What has been my most memorable experience of Easter?

Prayer

Risen Jesus, you shine on me with love flowing from your whole body, mind, and heart. You reach out your hand to welcome me into peace and renewed energy. You prepare me for my own future resurrection and invite me to share all this Good News with everyone I know and meet. I will sing your praises forever. I will tell our story everywhere. Worthy are you to receive honor, power, and glory forever and ever. Amen.